How to Outwit Any Auto, Truck, or RV Dealer *Every Time*

A Guide to Auto, Truck, and Recreational Vehicle Buying Techniques

JD Gallant

RV Consumer Group
Quilcene, Washington

How to Outwit any Auto, Truck, or RV Dealer *Every Time*

RV Consumer Group
Box 520 • Quilcene, WA 98376
(360) 765-3846 • Fax (360) 765-3233
Website at http://www.rv.org

Library of Congress Cataloging-in-Publication Data

Gallant, JD
[They're All Crooks!]
How to Outwit any Auto, Truck, or RV Dealer *Every Time* :
A Guide to Auto & RV Buying / JD Gallant.
p. cm.
Originally published: They're All Crooks! Quilcene, WA :
Quill Pub., 1994.
ISBN 1-890049-02-6
1. Automobiles--Purchasing. 2. Trucks--Purchasing.
3. Recreational Vehicles--Purchasing. I. Title.
TL162.G352 1997
629.222'029'6--dc21 97-32060
CIP

NOTICE

The information in this book is designed to guide—not to direct. It is strictly opinion based on personal experiences and research. It is the author's intention to correct any inaccuracies by periodically providing new editions and notices of any error. The author or publisher assumes no responsibilities for inconveniences or damages resulting from the use of this material. All users are encouraged to use this book in the manner for which it is intended.

Printed in the United States of America

About the Author

JD Gallant has been an RV enthusiast and RV trekker for over 35 years. Besides loving the fun and adventures of RVing, he has actively worked as a technical writer, teacher, auto and RV salesperson, and consultant for many years. Through his books, seminars, and workshops he has been instrumental in raising the awareness level of consumers when searching, buying, and using their autos, trucks, and RVs.

JD is co-founder and president of RV Consumer Group, a nonprofit organization dedicated to consumer education. He has authored other books including *The Green Book—RVs Rated, The Language of RVing*, and *How to Buy an RV Without Getting Ripped-off!*

Acknowledgements

This book could not have been produced without the assistance of a great staff and the magnificent administrative, artistic, and editorial skills of my wonderful and ever patient wife Connie.

The enthusiastic support of Roy Easton and Glenn Sharp throughout the years has been greatly responsible for keeping the organization machinery hurdling unbelievable obstacles. Their fidelity to the cause deserves the highest praise.

The dedication of attorney Brian Youngberg, a volunteer legal advisor, will always be appreciated. My son Jeff has been extremely helpful in legal research for all aspects of publishing and vehicle-related safety issues. The overall assistance of Jacque Hartley smoothed what would have been many rough roads. With my many other duties to attend to, Tom Liston's help allowed me needed time for the many rewrites and editing sessions required. Peggy Liston's support of administrative work has given our staff many breathers. The enthusiasm and skill of our webmasters, Tom and Judy Brown, has provided us with an opportunity to spread our message to the entire world through Internet.

To those mentioned and all others who have given me support in a variety of ways, I can only say, thank you - you are the greatest!

jd gallant

How to Outwit
any Auto, Truck, or RV Dealer
Every Time

Contents

Introduction

As you go through this book, some of you will think that I'm a bit hard on dealers. Those who've learned the hard way, however, have told me that I'm not hard enough. I have been told that dealer tactics are getting worse—not better. I have been given examples that are mind-boggling. I have seen the figures.

The hardest thing for most people to admit is that they've been taken. It appears as if consumers are so set on trusting people that they are blinded by some sense of false morality. And, it is false. Any time you allow someone to cheat you repeatedly, you are hurting yourself, your family, and your community. If you believe in turning the other cheek to financial abuse, you are reading the message incorrectly.

We've all heard that "trust must be earned." That message, however, seems to be forgotten in auto buying. I don't claim to know why, but I find that most people who I advise on buying techniques are reluctant to adhere to that simple message.

The message I'm sending in this book is clear: You can't trust the auto and RV industries to furnish you with a consistently good vehicle at a consistently good fair-market price. I honestly believe that these industries are so bedded with greed that there's no place for trust under the covers.

This is not to say that everyone in the auto and RV industries is dishonest. Quite to the contrary, I believe the majority of individuals in these industries are also basically honest citizens. I believe most who work in these industries are forced to change colors as soon as they punch the clock. They are forced to compromise their principles. They are forced to adhere to rules they may not like. Salespeople are told to get with it or get out. It's a dog-eat-dog arena.

If this book does one thing, I hope it makes you aware that you can make a deal—which means getting the right vehicle for the right price—only if you take off the blinders. The only way you're going to make a good investment in a safe vehicle is to stop, look, and listen. The only way you're going to protect your hard-earned dollars when buying an auto or RV is to lead with your brain, not with your heart. The only way you're going to get the best deal possible is to treat the person with whom you're dealing as your enemy—not your friend.

You may need the auto and RV industries, but they need *you* much more.

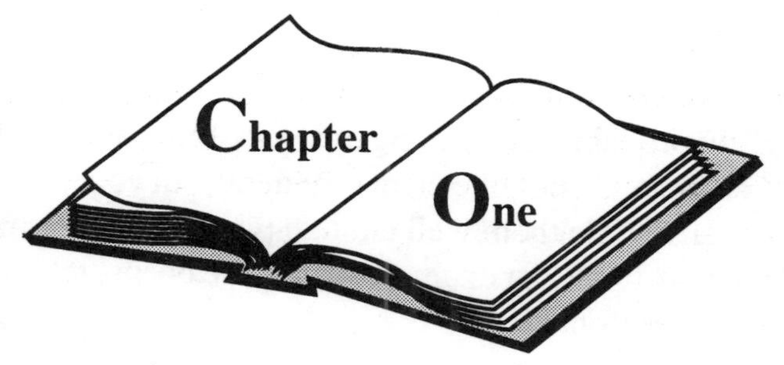

Learn How Dealers Work

You probably have strong opinions about auto dealers. You might not like them in general, but you think you can handle them well enough when it's necessary to deal. You may think, for example, that those boring television commercials will have an influence on the other guy—but not on you. Don't kid yourself. Auto dealers know how to influence you through advertising. They watch the advertising and the results. They pump out promo-ads and watch the dollar returns. For every $100 spent on a promo-ad, they expect to sit one prospect at the closing desk.

You just come in and ask for Old Bob and I'll show you deals like you've never seen before. I've got new and used cars and trucks that you can get into from $50 to $260 a month with no down. Me and my friendly tiger, Stripes, will take good care of you. Come in today. Ask for Old Bob.

"How can this be?" you ask. *"They sell their cars for only $100 over invoice. Where do they make the money?"* This question will be answered again and again throughout this book, but let me assure you that automobile dealers are making much more than $100 when they sell a car. Most dealers average a profit equal to at least 10 percent of the sticker price. That's $1,500 on a $15,000 car or truck. On many sales, they make much more.

My goal throughout this book will be to make you aware that every auto dealership is out to get you. I want to convince you that every dirty trick performed at a dealership is sanctioned by the dealership. It is my intention that by the time you finish this book you'll be ready to take on any dealership and end up with a good deal. To accomplish this end, however, you must understand the business practices to which most dealerships adhere.

The history of consumer manipulation began in the 1930s when auto dealerships began designing systems to bring customers in and keep them coming back. When World War II ended, dealers made millions by selling cars and trucks to an auto-starved public. As supply caught up with demand in the 1950s, catching buyers quickly became the issue. In-house systems converted to industry-wide systems. It was the beginning of system houses.

System houses were built on an inventory of dirty tricks. They had one goal: to put bodies in cars. As greed took over, they cared less for the consumer. They cared less for the community. They cared less for the salesperson. Everybody fit in a slot. For the unwary buyer, that slot was the driver's seat of an overpriced vehicle.

System houses became crooked. Although some were closed down by the law or lost their franchises, the nomadic salesperson carried the infection to the smaller dealerships who took some of the techniques to heart. These dealerships began to see advantages of buyer manipulation. As television entered the scene, dealers found it easier to take the American car buyer to the cleaners. With the development of computers, the industry took con-

trol of its own people—just as it had done with the consumer.

The only thing that consumers have going for them is the Monroney Act, named after Senator Mike Monroney. This federal legislation has forced auto manufacturers to have a consistent price sheet pasted on every automobile. The Monroney sticker was forced upon the auto industry because of the dirty tricks and other abuses heaped upon the consumer.

Although the Monroney sticker works for some, most consumers still trust the system. They don't see the Monroney sticker because salespeople have learned how to manipulate around it. Salespeople have developed techniques of turning screws so gently that the buyer thinks he's getting a massage.

Each technique that works for the dealership is brought into the system. Selling has become a team effort. At weekly sales meetings the managers educate, inspire, and coerce the sales force. Spiffs, bonuses, vacations, and gifts are given generously for sales performance. The salespeople become big spenders and smooth operators. It's dictated teamwork—and it works. Every salesperson is allowed to develop his own techniques for applying dirty tricks as long as he operates within the system—which tolerates no dissention.

"Tell 'em you love 'em, then sock it to 'em," is the new

GO
TEAM!

You hit them at the knees and I'll take it from there.

battle cry. It's now dog-eat-dog and all dogs eat buyers.

Those in the auto industry who don't like the system-house mentality—or the control mechanism that goes with it—leave system dealerships for the freedom of smaller dealerships or used car lots. Although some of these salespeople and managers are dedicated to servicing the customer, these are few. Most who leave the system are infected enough to carry the system's techniques wherever they go. These techniques are disastrous to the buyer when he is caught unaware.

We have a low overhead so we pass the savings on to you.

You'll find used car lots and small dealerships giving the impression that they can sell for less. In most cases this is a ploy. An aggressive consumer can successfully skirmish with a big dealership as well as a small dealership.

It's important to realize that your strength as a buyer must be carried all the way through the process. If you let your guard down, you're going to lose thousands of dollars and add untold hours of frustration to your life. You need to keep your guard up because hot-shot salespeople in the auto industry care for nothing except their commissions. They'll do anything for a sale. They'll lie through smiling lips. They'll treat you to every dirty trick they know—and there are many.

Hot-shot salespeople are good at what they do. They know

how to write the ads to get you moving to their dealership. They are superb at manipulating you into a vehicle that will give them a big profit. They are experts at getting you emotionally involved during a presentation. They are cunning at devising ways to sit you at their desk. They are velvety smooth at getting you into a closing situation. They are divisive at getting a trade-in away from you at a fraction of its cash value. They are heartless when milking you for more than you want to give.

Preeeesenting...

A hot-shot salesperson will begin his act much like that of the circus ringmaster. He wants to see you happy. He wants to see you smiling. He wants to see you clapping. He wants to control your emotions.

The goal of a hot-shot salesperson is to get you excited. He'll show you features and benefits that are guaranteed to satisfy your needs and wants. He'll have his lines down pat. He'll know exactly what to say for every response you give. He'll bend to your every mood and attitude. A hot-shot salesperson will know where he's taking you within 15 minutes. If you can imagine yourself being invited to a circus and then enticed to enter the lion's cage, you will have a good picture of auto dealing with a hot-shot salesperson—who from now on we'll call Smoothy.

Auto dealers have justified their arsenals of dirty tricks and manipulative techniques because of the public's antagonistic behavior toward auto salespeople. Since you need the dealership to give you choices in types, makes, and brands, you must learn to negotiate without an antagonistic attitude. Although there is little in the industry to trust, you must learn

to communicate with the system. When you learn how they play the game, you will be able to use them instead of allowing them to use you.

You don't need a military tank to skirmish with a Smoothy. What you need is basic information and lots of determination. You need only to become a smart, friendly, and stubborn consumer. You must be prepared to meet the salesperson assigned to the front line—the person whose primary objective will be to get you into a vehicle that will pay him or her a good commission. This expert will attempt to push enough of your buy-buttons to get you to negotiate. If you are not prepared, this person will get you to his desk—a place where the system can take over.

To beat the dealership you must skirmish only so far, retreat, then return at a time of your choosing. You must have a strategy, and you must keep it simple. You must have a purpose each time you visit a dealership, and you must resolve to limit your visit to that purpose.

To effectively skirmish with the auto sales system, you're

going to have to do one thing that will be slightly alien to your lovable nature. You're going to have to look into a smiling face and think, *"I don't trust you."*

When this friendly person starts to probe with small-talk, you're going to make yourself ignore the sincere questioning and say, *"You know, I'm very excited about seeing some of your cars."* When the salesperson tries to get you involved in a road test, you'll pleasantly refuse until you are quite convinced that the vehicle is worth considering. When he says, *"I can get you some figures if you'll come with me,"* you won't follow him to the desk. When he wants to introduce you to another salesperson or sales manager, you'll politely tell him that you appreciate the assistance, but you must leave. You're going to tell him this because it's the truth. It's the truth because if you stay you'll be breaking a pledge to which you must adhere. This simple pledge is: **I will not negotiate until I know exactly what I want and how much it will cost me.** Making this pledge part of your life will save you thousands of dollars.

I'll trust you if
you'll trust me.

To adhere to this pledge, you must not trust any member of the dealership's sales staff. Your trust must be directed toward your own ingenuity to survive the many barriers and pitfalls that the dealer will use against you. You must come to the realization that giving your trust to a salesperson will destroy your control of the purchase.

Manipulative tricks are inherent to the auto sales arena. You have surely seen many of the tricks that have been pulled on automobile consumers by service stations, garages, used car lots, and dealers. These tricks are so common that consumer advocates have their files bulging with specifics. We hear about the same scam happening again and again. The scam gets publicity, dies down a bit, then pops up to grab the next generation. Although not every scam associated with autos started with auto or RV dealerships, most find their way into one.

The "repair-scare" scam has been working for decades. In some dealerships, it's so subtle that the victim never knows he's been caught. The first time I witnessed the repair-scare scam, it was pulled on an older woman who brought her car

This little ball joint represents the true condition of your car. The entire suspension is shot. I can fix this part for $300 but I'm not sure the rest of it is safe or will last you very long. What you really need is a new car.

into the dealership because it was using too much oil. The chief mechanic scared her into buying another car by telling her the engine was shot. I heard him bragging, *"She ate it like a piece of cake. Hell, all it needs is a one-dollar breather tube and five minutes time. I've been promised the car for four hundred bucks."*

I've seen mechanics scare women to a point of panic because of exaggeration of front-end or brake repair. Fifty percent of the time these women end up talking with a salesperson. Most of them are sold another car with big profits for the dealership. The mechanic always gets a few bucks in cash for his unscrupulous behavior. It happens to both men and women. It could easily happen to you.

Scams aren't easy to document. If it involves a trade, the evidence is gone minutes after the papers are signed. If caught, many dealers will put the blame on an employee—going as far as firing the person then hiring him back a few days later.

Scams are especially effective on "lay-downs." (Lay-downs are buyers who are so easy to manipulate they are considered the first car of the gravy train.) It is commonplace for salespeople to fight over these prospects. When you realize that gross profits on lay-downs easily average 30 percent, you can understand their value to the first salesperson who reaches them.

The reason the profits are so good is that lay-downs are either extremely trusting or have an urgent need. Even when they demand their $200 over invoice, they get laid away. Lay-downs don't know the facts of auto dealing. Lay-downs don't see the shell game for what it is.

A lay-down is especially subject to the shell game. Lay-downs are blind to the subtle changing of the figures on the worksheet or on the contract. Lay-downs are easily convinced that the over-allowance on the trade is a generous concession by the dealer. Lay-downs don't know that ACV means actual cash value—and they very possibly think they don't need to

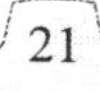

Lay-downs!
Easy-sell!
Gee, this looks like a nice place to buy a car.

know. Lay-downs are naturally trusting or easily converted.

Every auto salesperson dreams of getting at least one lay-down a month. Two lay-downs will make them ecstatic. Auto and RV salespeople easily make $1,000 or more commission on a lay-down.

An "easy-sell" is about the same as a lay-down except they're not as obvious up front. Most buyers are easy-sells. Unlike lay-downs, easy-sells might be tight-mouthed during the qualifying session. They might even be distrustful as they tour the inventory. But when the right vehicle flashes before their eyes, easy-sells are turned on. They get emotional. The salesperson gets buying signals all over the place. He says, *"Let's go for a demonstration ride,"* and the easy-sell jumps in the driver's seat. When the salesperson talks about power or economy, the easy-sell nods more than he questions. When the salesperson tells him to pull into the "sold car" area, the easy-sell doesn't feel pressured—he feels good. When the salesperson sits him down at the desk, *"to see what we can do in figures,"* the easy-sell quickly accepts a cup of coffee or cold beverage. When the salesperson talks about, *"buying today,"* the easy-sell nods and says, *"If the deal is right, maybe."*

Auto dealerships have perfected the skill of leading the customer, and easy-sells are easy to lead. They are not unlike the proverbial sheep comforted by the presence of someone who appears to be a protector. They don't mind being led because without help they'd be lost. Easy-sells know that auto dealerships are full of wolves—but their salesperson is always an exception.

Salespeople behave well with easy-sells. They will take their time and count their commissions. The lay-down is the cake; the easy-sell is the frosting.

To not be a lay-down or an easy-sell, you've got to realize that all salespeople come from the same mold. They have been trained by the best trainers in the world. They have been recruited into a system that perpetuates itself through extensive training. Whether these dealerships are large or small, whether they are haggle-free or wheeler-dealers, they think the same way.

Any normal human being who works at an auto dealership for more than six months has been corrupted. They will defend and justify much of the system although not necessarily all of it. Although not every salesperson is a crook or plays the scam game, you must consider that every salesperson at an auto dealership is part of a team that generally functions as crooks, practices scams, and maintains an inventory of dirty tricks.

Salespeople learn to manipulate. Every sales book, every sales video, every sales course, every sales seminar, and every sales workshop teaches salespeople to manipulate the prospect. I have never seen a sales program to the contrary.

Manipulation by the salesperson may be subtle, but it's there. You, as an auto buyer, must see the auto sales arena for what it is. You must see that the mold has been cast. Every salesperson you meet will try to lead you to his desk. Every salesperson will try to close you today. He's been trained to do just that. Let's see if in the next four chapters I can convince you to resist that manipulation.

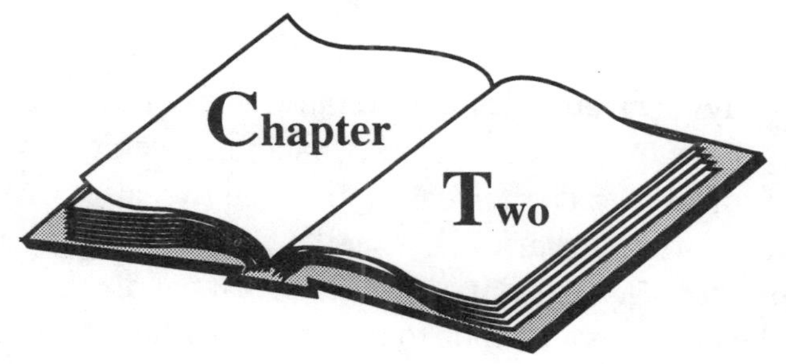

Stay Within Your Budget

Buying an auto would be relatively simple if you didn't have to finance it. Since financing a vehicle through the dealer is often easy, you need to realize that auto dealers get rich because they handle financing. They make loan sharks look like saints. They don't just handle the financing—they use it as a weapon to cut you into little pieces. If you don't give them this weapon, they can't use it against you.

This section is designed to convince you to set specific limits on total spending—which must include the cost of financing. My goal is to get you to leave the subject of financing behind until all other details are settled. You need to find the right vehicle before you discuss financing. You need to get to the bottom price before you discuss financing. You need to check alternate sources before you discuss financing. Although you should know your capability for financing before you get too involved in shopping, you must keep the details away from the salesperson.

By taking this much from your budget for a new car you'll be cutting your repair bills to almost nothing. Doesn't this make sense to you?
BUDGET

You probably think dealer financing is a service to help you buy a vehicle. Wrong! It is not a service to help you in any way. It's a service designed to help the dealer get more profits from the sale. The prime motive for the dealer to help you with financing is to get more money from you—to break your budget.

Breaking your budget is automatic. Auto salespeople think "commission" whenever they give any advice. They must think this way because their livelihood depends on the profit in the deal. Financing is a tool to help get those commissions—which come from your hard earnings. But auto dealers have to get you onto the lot to work their game. They're experts at working ads and promotions to get you into their dealership. They need a captive audience so they can work their manipulations. They know how to put a television production together and assemble words for a local newspaper. They've done it hundreds of times and they know the success rate. It's a system that's not easy to beat.

This is the same model at $600 less. And look, the payment is $40 less than what we were quoted.

The system, however, can be beat. With a bit of knowledge and desire to control your pursestrings, you'll automatically scrutinize the "fine print" of special deals. Eventually you'll learn how to set a deal in motion in your favor. During the process of shopping, you'll probably come across more than one attractive deal. You will see ads designed solely to get you in. When you get to the dealership, you might even come across a "bait-and-switch game" in motion. It won't be at all what it seemed to be. The car will be there, but it will have limited options and colors - nothing you'll want. And to get the lower payment as advertised will require a much larger down. You'll find a lot of pressure. They'll do almost anything for you if you'll buy "today." You'll decide to leave, but in leaving you'll notice that most of the closing booths are full. There will be many buyers taking advantage of the "sale."

When *you* go to any dealership to look around, they'll try to close you on the same day. They'll expect you to look around—and get caught. Most people get caught because they know how to work the emotions. As soon as they find out that you are financing the purchase, they'll talk payments. A Smoothy will get you so excited you'll see yourself as an owner. Smoothy will help you see the car in your driveway or driving down the highway.

Bob, this model has the power you need. Mary, would payments of about $350 a month be just about right for your budget?
Yes, I think I could handle that.
Of course, I can take your present car for a trade. Do you ....

Auto salespeople are good at distracting prospects from their needs and working on their wants. They're great at convincing prospects that they can afford whatever they want. If the salesperson discovers how you intend to finance, he will begin qualifying you to find out how far he can take you. He will subtly ask you enough questions to form a strategy. He will get a profit figure in his mind and work you on that. He might even convince you to switch to a lesser vehicle because he can make more profit on the deal. If you are a payment buyer, his strategy is already set in concrete. He knows where he'll be taking you.

It ain't what I wanted, but it sure is fun.

Salespeople want payment buyers so they can control the profit. When they control financing, they have hundreds of opportunities for milking the prospect to the very last drop. Most auto salespeople are cruelly indifferent to the buyer. You must assume that your salesperson is no different.

Of all the car, truck, and RV buyers that I've interviewed and talked to, most ended up buying a vehicle other than what they went in to buy. When asked, *"Why?"* they had no answer. At the time of the purchase they were convinced that the vehicle shown was the best for them. They somehow felt that the salesperson had their interest at heart.

Of course, it is impossible for a salesperson to think of your budget and safety ahead of his commissions. An auto salesperson works for an industry that is known for consumer indifference. The auto dealer's reputation equals that of the Mafia. Almost every auto salesperson has developed his own "kiss of death."

"Ridiculous," you say, *"it can't be that bad."*

It is that bad. I'll tell you one story that's very close to home. A friend of mine went in to have her European car repaired and got caught in the service department. She was sold an American fancy four-wheel drive with the European car taken on trade. The dealer was asking $21,000 and gave her an exciting allowance for her trade.

The vehicle she was sold was four years old with 65,000 miles on the odometer. It originally sold new for about $24,000. Although the asking price was just over $20,000, the Kelley Blue Book wholesale value was under $10,000. Even with an attractive trade-in allowance, this intelligent young lady lost $5,000 because she trusted a car salesperson. She believed that, like a grocery store, prices are pretty much standard. Of course, this is hogwash. An asking price is made for dealing. It has no relationship to real value.

Since you cannot buy the right car, truck, or RV without shopping, you better learn to take the auto salesperson for what he is. There is no way you can avoid this approach under the current rules of the game. Because the current system will be with us for a while yet, why not learn to cope with it? It's really quite easy. All you need to do is concentrate on the mentality of the auto salesperson and follow a few simple rules. Remember the pledge you took? **I will not negotiate until I know exactly what I want and how much it will cost me.** Now, take this second pledge: **I will not talk finances until all other conditions are settled.** Get these two simple rules of auto buying in your brain. Memorize them or put them in bold print on the first page of your note pad.

As I mentioned before, auto salespeople have lots of help in manipulating the buyer. For example, a good salesperson is taught that he never says, *"contract."* It's always, *"agreement"* or *"paperwork."* He never says, *"buy."* It's *"invest."* He never says *"used."* It's *"pre-owned."* He never says, *"Sign here.*" It's "*Okay this,*" or "*Give me your approval here.*" There are turn-on words and turn-off words. Good salespeople learn to avoid turn-off words and use turn-on words just as they learn manipulative tricks.

An auto salesperson learns new tricks all the time because the system perpetuates itself. Because you have the ultimate power in your fingers, you can skirmish with salespeople and win. It will only happen, however, if you have a system of your own.

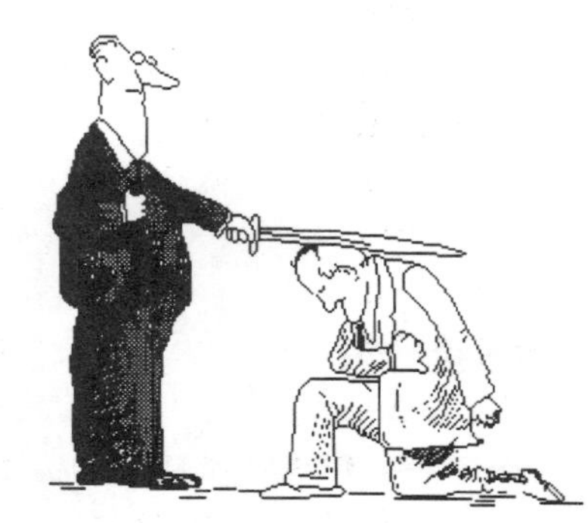

I knight you Sir Gooblygook for saving the deal by using great words like special, save, beauty, clean, sale, cozy, efficient, powerful, spacious, luxurious, elegant, investment, initial investment, agreement, and today.

Not everyone can pay cash for a vehicle. Most of us require financing. If you finance the purchase, you will make monthly payments on the purchase price and the interest. To understand the financing package you'll need to do some research.

Your first financing objective will be to determine how much each $100 borrowed will cost you in payments. To do this you must visit or call a credit union or bank for current interest rates and number of months on new and used. Get at least two sets of figures. When you find out how much you might have to spend, you can get the exact terms and payments. It'll take some work, but you'll be saving hundreds or even thousands of dollars.

If you apply with the credit union or bank and get turned down, you should discuss the reason with the finance officer. You need to know the problem in case you want to take it further. You must keep in mind, however, that you'll pay a premium for financing if your credit isn't good. With poor credit you'll pay more for the vehicle, you'll get less for the trade, you'll be pressured more for insurances, and you'll pay a higher interest rate.

Getting a figure for each $100 with the specific terms you need will make it easy for you to estimate payments when you get your figures on the purchase. This frees you from tying financing into the deal. You should get some sort of pre-approval if you can. The more you can do on your own, the more money you will save. Remember, a dollar saved is ten dollars earned.

Sorry. Your debt-to-income ratio is 40 percent, you've had some problems with payments, and you've only been on that job for two years. I would only consider the loan with 25 percent down.

There's always someone who'll see things differently.

If you make the decision to go for dealer financing, you should brace yourself for tricks of the trade—tricks designed to get more out of you than you think you are paying. A very successful salesperson has a trick of covering the real figures with an arm or hand as he passes the pen. He'll say with a smile: *"Just press hard as you okay it here. I want you to be able to read your copy."* You don't see the real figures because he's playing the shell game while being a nice guy.

Total amount to be paid:
$26,468.96

Recently one of my students was closing a deal when he discovered that the contract was for $2,000 more than the negotiated amount. The response by the finance manager to the *"Why?"* was simple and direct. *"The owner won't let the deal go through the way it is,"* he said. *"This is the best we can do."* This was after the deal was accepted by the sales manager. Most of these "changes" aren't caught.

Another student had such a good deal on a used RV that he rushed it through the finance office. He was surprised to find out later that he owed the dealership $500 because the payoff on the trade had been "estimated" too low. The trick was simple. The finance manager wrote the payoff low to show more equity so that he could get the loan approved for a higher amount. You'd be surprised how many people find out too late how much the entire deal is costing them. They miss the final step and take a costly tumble.

Some of you will begin to trust the salesperson during your shopping then carry that trust into the closing room. This is foolhardy. Too many people tell me, *"But JD, he was so nice. He was honest up front, and he didn't pressure me at all."* Right!

Being nice up front is the way to sell cars, trucks, and RVs. Being smooth and nice is the way to conduct a presentation. Being candid and casual is the way to get you into the closing booth. The perception of no pressure is the way to keep you from walking away. The salesperson's creed is: *Use pressure only when the prospect is walking or when there's little profit in the deal.* If you don't get pressure from a salesperson, you're doing something very wrong.

Hey! Just a little bit more.

Salespeople know they have to treat the prospect like royalty to get profit. The more the profit, the smoother they get. You can't have it both ways. If you are determined to be treated like a long-lost relative, you better leave the shopping to someone else. If you need smiles and attention from a salesperson to get down to business, expect to pay through the nose every time you see the ivory.

Once you leave the dealership, the salesperson and managers won't care about your problems. You might receive a card sent by the system in hopes of getting you back again. You might even receive a phone call from the system to get you to further their cause by giving referrals. All of this proves that you've left them too much money. To them, you're just a piece of meat on a hook.

An obvious payment buyer is a salesperson's dream prospect. The program is already set to bump a payment buyer to another car or to higher payments. Payment buyers are not a serious challenge to a good salesperson.

The payment buyer's primary focus is on the payment. They might want a specific car if it fits into the payment. They will take almost any term if it fits into the payment. They will take any deal if the payment is right. Payment buyers are usually easy-sells. They are almost guaranteed to give the dealer big gross profits.

You do not have to be a payment buyer just because you finance your purchase. Good auto buyers are value buyers. They compare the price to the quality. Whether you finance or not, you need to be a value buyer.

Don't let an auto or RV salesperson turn you into a payment buyer. They all try to do it. Right after the greeting they'll ask how you're going to pay. They'll talk about payments. During the presentation, they'll mention payments and they'll continue to make an issue during the close. If they can convert you to a payment buyer, their job of manipulating the price, the trade, and the financing terms will be much easier.

If you give the salesperson the fixed amount of dollars you can spend, he can easily convert the figure to payments. Once he finds your needs and wants, he'll have you pegged. Giving him a fixed expenditure allows him to manipulate you in grand style.

Because you're smarter than most, you are not going to leave one penny more than you have to with a dealer. What you pay will be *your* decision. Because a dealer wants to deal, you'll deal—but you'll keep control. You won't talk financing until you find the vehicle that fits your budget and transportation needs. You won't let sweet talk keep you from this course. You'll ignore qualifying questions unless they relate to finding the vehicle you want.

When the salesperson asks you, *"How long have you owned your present car?"* you'll ignore the question because the answer might tell him whether you bought it new or used. When he asks, *"What price range would fit in your budget?"* you'll say, *"I'll know when I see the right car."* You'll be telling him nothing. If he asks, *"Are you planning on trading your car?"* you'll say, *"Maybe."* You'll keep smiling and looking—while telling the salesperson nothing.

Only after you get figures that are within your guidelines on the total amount will you be ready to answer specific questions. If you are pre-approved for financing, all you need to do is tell the salesperson that you are pre-approved and that you might be interested if the *bottom line* is satisfactory. He or she has heard this before, so don't expect much of a reaction. The dealer's plan of action is always to bump you on the deal and bump you on the financing. Dealers are superb at doing just that.

You, however, will have your figures. You'll stand firm as they try to bump you and turn you. You'll stay within your budget.

We want the station wagon for $14,800 and we won't pay over $280 a month.

There comes a time to stand like the Rock of Gibraltar.

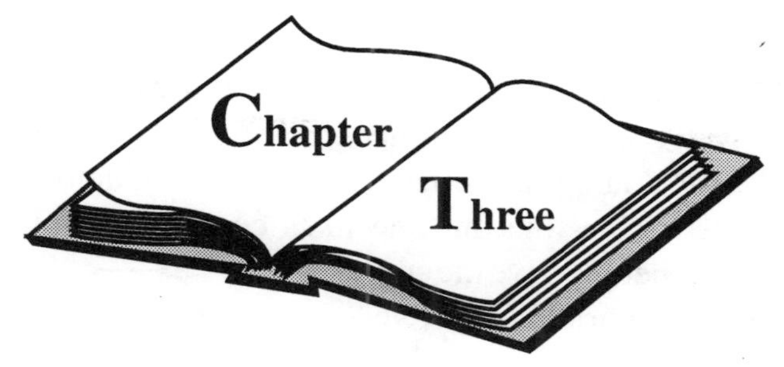

Make Research Fun & Profitable

The reason auto dealers get rich is that most people won't do the research needed to find a good car, truck, or RV at a good price. Another reason auto and RV dealers get rich is that no one likes confessing to being a sucker. Few people have the courage to tell the world that they've been taken to the cleaners. If no one talks about the problems of auto dealing, how are people going to know the kind of losses they are facing? It won't get better for any of us until we decide to clean it up.

Wow! I better look some more.

Now let's get motivated by a fact: A good researcher will, on the average, get a 7 percent better deal than a buyer who won't do serious research. This is about $1,000 on a $15,000 deal. Many buyers throw away this much money every time they buy a vehicle. Some throw away much more. That $5,000 overpaid by my friend represented the savings of six years of hard work. How long does it take you to save $2,000? $3,000? $5,000? How many days are you willing to dedicate to save this kind of money?

Most of you think that the most you're going to lose is a few hundred bucks. That's malarkey. To a dealer a few hundred bucks is a small bump. Those of you who've heard about paying only $200 or $300 over invoice are hearing the *Star Spangled Banner*— the opening song. What you need to hear is *Good Night Ladies*—the closing tune. Between the opening song and the closing tune you're going to have to do a lot of dancing to get a good deal. If you don't do the dancing, you'll never get the prize.

Every auto buyer would like to be able to avoid the research necessary for a good deal. Every auto buyer knows that if he could find just one honest dealer he could avoid the work. But finding that one honest dealer appears to be a pipe dream. Even if a small percent of auto dealers are basically honest, we can't know which are honest until we do our research.

This cherry just came in on trade. I'm not supposed to show you this, but here's the purchase agreement to show you how much we paid for it. We allowed 13 grand. You might be able to get it for under 10 grand if you buy today. Isn't it a beauty?

Auto dealers learn their techniques well. They practice manipulative tricks every day. They have the best teachers in the world. They learn from each other while developing similar characteristics and techniques. Do you really think you can match this type of experience?

Auto dealers have developed tricks to use on each other, on financing institutions, on auto manufacturers, and on their own salespeople. Do you really think they won't use tricks on you?

Manufacturers are in the business for profit. They have produced dozens of seriously flawed models and have never shown remorse for the lives and savings lost. They have been forced into producing safer and more efficient vehicles by consumer groups and the government. Do you really think it's now safe to trust them?

The answers are obvious. The auto industry is fully outfitted for mortal combat with the consumer. They will not give up their weapons while they are winning every battle. Your only chance of getting a good deal is to have your own offensive and defensive plans in place. You have no other choice

Dealers have plenty of tricks to waylay those who aren't fully prepared. Most of these tricks are designed to stimulate buying "today." Salespeople learn to ask questions like *"If I can...will you buy today?"* Enticements may be an attractive payment, a special price, or a temporary rebate. The sales pitch may include an explanation of why a vehicle can be sold at an "unbelievable" price. It may be there's an attractive interest rate for a limited time. It may be that the salesperson will suggest that he can get more for your trade "today."

The salesperson will gain your trust with deceptive tactics.

He justifies this deceptiveness as part of the game. He doesn't feel dishonest because he believes you are dishonest. There's a saying among auto salespeople that goes, *"Dealers are cheaters and buyers are liars."* Such a statement reinforces the salesperson's conviction that the only way he can win is to go for blood.

Ah ha! Just as I thought. He said this van would pull a 5,000 pound trailer but the towing guide says that with the three-to-one axle ratio it will pull only 3,000 pounds.

As the game gets played, you are caught up in a win or lose situation. You will be fighting a strategy built over decades. You will win only if you know how to respond.

To play the game you must prepare and practice. Having talked to many people who have played, I've found that those who have lost were not prepared. The tie games were a result of the buyer being partially prepared and partially lucky. Those who rely on luck and gut feeling almost always lose. A toss of the coin is still fifty-fifty.

Make your research a pleasant adventure by treating yourself to a reward for the good job you're doing. After all, you'll be earning at least $100 an hour for the time spent, so the cost of a pizza treat is nothing. When you take a day off to do your research, treat yourself to a meal at a good restaurant.

During active research keep

your energy level stable with high-protein foods. Since coming off a sugar or caffeine high will make you feel tired, do not indulge in sweets and be careful about too much coffee. If you don't eat right, your resistance will be low. A good salesperson will sense your urgency to get the purchase done with and go into high gear. When you start weakening, he'll put on the pressure. Good food and a good attitude will help you keep control.

By now you know that dealing for a car, truck, or RV is an adventure. It is not unlike climbing a mountain or sailing the rough seas. It is not unlike putting together a Thanksgiving dinner for the entire clan. It is not unlike planning a car trip across the United States. All of these things take research and preparation. But all these things cost money while a research adventure will save you thousands of dollars. This is an adventure you can afford.

Your research is also a test of your ability to communicate. You'll find that communicating with few words will get better results than talking your head off. You'll learn that listening is essential. If you listen more and say little, you'll drive salespeople crazy.

Don't be intimidating or pushy. If a salesperson thinks you're a lost cause, he'll either shun you or blow you out. Either way you'll lose. Because you need his or her help to get basic information, you must make the salesperson work for you.

Your first objective during the research mode will be to get the salesperson to think of you as a valuable prospect that should not be pushed into a "buy today" routine. This is usually quite easy. Since you need his attention for at least twenty minutes, you'll need to be subtle and organized in your questions and answers.

You want the salesperson to think of you as a discriminating buyer who is eager to find the right vehicle— but not necessarily today. Because the salesperson has been well-trained to deal with this scenario, he should go into a good presentation while building rapport. This is exactly what you want. As you write notes in a small notebook or in a brochure, you'll begin to feel that you have control. Once a salesperson invests time in you, he'll hang on.

Your second objective will be to control the research process. This won't be easy because the salesperson will have firm instructions to get you to his desk. As you go into each dealership you will be attempting to collect brochures. If you are buying a van or a truck for towing, always request a towing guide. In some dealerships you might have to ask a salesperson for the relevant booklets. This is a good time to let him or her know that you are a serious shopper. If a salesperson is truly professional, he or she will give you a brief presentation of the product and the dealership. Try to get the presentation in the showroom display to prevent being pressured in the sales lot. It is usually best to avoid a demonstration ride on your research visits.

Making a statement like, *"I'm going to need a car,"* is much better than, *"I need a car."* The latter tells the salesperson that the issue of urgency exists. If this happens, he will go into a trial-close mode rather than a presentation mode. This is counterproductive to your research.

Try not to ask for information that is in the brochure. Although I've talked quite a bit about the auto salesperson's training, I must tell you that very little of it involves the technical aspects of the vehicle. Ninety-five percent of an auto or RV salesperson's training involves sales techniques while five percent is about the product. Do not rely on salespeople for technical knowledge. Use brochures and consumer guides. After finding out that the salesperson's information was inaccurate, many buyers have said to me: *"But, JD, he was so helpful."* Wrong information given by a salesperson is never helpful to a buyer.

You've been so helpful, but what I really need to know is the amount of weight the Fleetline can carry in the trunk and then—

Do not let the dealership's attitude get to you. Make it respond to your needs. As a franchised dealership they have the obligation to help you make the right decision. Don't let the dealership get to you through intimidation or indifference. Stick to your guns. It's your money. It's your time.

Everyone knows that getting an auto salesperson to talk with a straight tongue is almost impossible. Most auto salespeople will say what you want them to say. They'll use the same words they've used on hundreds of prospects. They'll switch their lines to meet the buying signals. They'll omit when it increases the chance of higher profits. They'll stretch the truth when it strengthens their presentation. Most will lie whenever they can get by with lying. It is my opinion that less than 10 percent of auto salespeople are honest when on the job.

With this in mind, you should understand that words spoken about warranties have absolutely no value. You must read the warranty. Since this is a matter of public knowledge, the courts won't hang a dealer on what a salesperson promises with his tongue. Ask the salesperson to show you the warranty. Call the manufacturer if you need clarification.

Don't worry about the water leak, Mary, I'll take care of any problem.

As of 1985, Federal law requires a used vehicle to have a warranty statement on the window. Read it. In some states it becomes an implied warranty if the dealer fixes anything without charging you after the purchase has been consummated. You must be careful of the wording. There are words and phrases designed to mislead but are legally binding. Those who play with words know that most people are great scanners of the written word. Do not scan.

Taking a demonstration ride during the research mode might throw you off guard. Most of us buy a vehicle because the one we have is worn out. This means that almost anything we look at is going to be better than what we now have. It will run better, it will ride better, and it will handle better. The salesperson knows this. He knows that if he can get you excited about any vehicle, it will help you forget everything I'm saying. He wants to lower all barriers that might prevent him from making a good commission. If he sends you for a road test, he'll be taking his chances; but if he gives you a demonstration ride, he knows that he'll have a better chance of closing you today.

Don't ever begin to think that the salesperson has your interest at heart because he switches you to another vehicle. He might switch you because he's discovered something during his qualifying that will make him a bigger commission. Don't let the salesperson choose the vehicle for a road test or demonstration ride. It must be your choice.

You don't have to worry. This vehicle is practically guaranteed forever.

Notice how a salesperson gets you to pull into a special area in front of the salesroom when you return from the ride. This tactic is to get you into the "owner" frame of mind. He's an expert at getting you from the driver's seat to the seat by his desk.

Because cars, trucks, and RVs are technical machinery, it's easy to buy the wrong vehicle. You can't trust what the salesperson tells you and you can be sure the manufacturer won't give you all the facts. You must dig on your own for the right answers.

Salespeople are naturally reluctant to tell you anything negative about their products. They know that if they mention even the slightest negative you will remember it and forget everything else.

Salespeople know that such organizations as Consumer Reports exist but few of them ever bother to study the reports. They know that smart buyers check the ratings; so if an issue comes up, they will have an answer. *"Oh, there were a few problems, but those have been corrected,"* is a quick and effective answer to someone who is mesmerized by the trinkets and colors. Buyers who get excited don't want to get turned off.

Unsafe vehicles are built every day. Some buyers consider safety as relative. *"None are safe,"* they say. *"Some are just safer than others. This one gives me a sense of adventure."*

Salespeople know how the average buyer thinks. When showing a high-performance sports car, they use test questions like, *"Have you ever had the thrill of driving a car at 100 miles per hour?"* The answer tells them how to pound the nails.

Auto salespeople can tell scary stories about demonstration rides in unsafe vehicles. They take the risk with a stranger because the odds of getting certain types of people excited about a high-performance car are high. Once excited, such a buyer becomes putty in the hands of a skilled artist. Because every salesperson is on some sort of wage incentive, you cannot trust him with your life.

There is, of course, a logical reason for a salesperson to keep you from continuing your research. He knows that once you leave, there's a slim chance of ever seeing you again. He wants you inside where the system can eat you up. He'll go as far as he can then he'll turn you to another salesperson. Eventually, you'll have to go through the process; but during the research mode, you must avoid the desk.

As I've mentioned before, the success of your research will be your ability to sponge information without being led. *"I will need a car in the near future,"* will cool the salesperson down without putting out the flame. He can go back to the boss, shrug, and say, *"Just another shopper."* Sometimes the boss buys it—sometimes not. Some dealerships mandate a turnover. You can usually avoid a turnover in such dealerships by not entering the building. If you get caught inside, you must not sit at the desk. The desk is reserved for the day you deal.

If you do your research on a rainy day, expect to be labeled as a serious buyer. Shoppers do not enter auto dealerships when the weather is nasty. If you go for research when it's raining or snowing, you'll have to say up front that you are shopping for information. Even then you should be prepared for pressure.

Auto salespeople will have tactics to turn you from a shopper into a buyer. They've done it thousands of times before. They won't give up easily. During the research mode you must be prepared to use your feet instead of your seat.

I don't understand.
It had lots of power
on the road test.

If you are planning on using your car as a trade-in, you can bet the salesperson will find out. At least he'll try very hard. Any figure you get at this time won't be accurate. When he finds out that you're not buying today, he will give you a "highball" for the trade allowance and a "lowball" for the purchase price. The highball is more than he can give you for a trade and the lowball is less than he (or another dealer) can sell the vehicle for. Many salespeople feel that giving you an unworkable price is the only way to keep you from buying at the competition. Not all salespeople will do this, but many of them will.

If you show any inclination that your old car will be worked into the deal, the salesperson will definitely have a lot to say about its value today. He will try to find out if you are planning on using it as a down payment. He'll want to know how much you owe on it. If you give him any answer other than a shrug, you'll be starting the dealing process. You're not ready to buy. You're not ready to buy. You're not ready to buy. You're not ready to buy.

"I am not ready to buy today," you will say.

"If I give you $______ would you buy today?" he will ask.

"No!" you will say, *"I am not ready to buy today."*

If the salesperson pushes too much, he knows he may lose you. He must give in for now. He will take basic information and let you go. You will take your information and leave unscathed. That's good!

If you've ever had a car that went to the dogs before it wore out, you'll never forget it. Some cars lose their luster almost as soon as they leave the lot. As the paint fades and chips, you'll want to keep such a car parked in the back yard. You might find the upholstery showing wear and wheel covers beginning to rust long before it's paid for. Because the engine never sounds right, you won't be able to sell it on the open market. You will soon determine that it was a very bad buy.

Many cars are built to sell. The designers are influenced by the marketing staff that keeps one eye on the competition. Most marketers want glitter and cost cutting while most designers want substance. The marketers usually win.

To avoid buying a "dog" you need to study older vehicles of the same make and model. Take a day and travel the used car lots. Look at vehicles five to ten years old. If you relax and just look, you'll get an education. Do it on a Sunday right after noon and the salespeople will think you're out for a stroll. Don't take notes. Say, *"I'm just wandering."*

Good research will help you develop gut feeling for future

purchases. Good research is never wasted. Good research is a learning process that will strengthen your financial base for years in the future. It goes way beyond the current purchase. Each time will get better. Each time will be a learning experience. Each time your skills will get sharper. If you do good research and stick to brands that have a good reputation, life will be better.

Getting a lemon for a vehicle is like getting a sour grape at a party. It's like finding half a worm in an apple. It's like the feeling you get when you peel a rotten banana for your cereal. These are the kinds of feelings you could get if you become sloppy in your research.

No one's happy with a lemon

The legal definition of a lemon is somewhat vague and varies from state to state. Generally, however, if you take your (new) vehicle in during the warranty period a number of times with the same or similar complaints without satisfactory resolution of the complaint, you probably have a lemon. In some states this means that the manufacturer must replace the vehicle or reimburse you. It's not as simple as it sounds, but if you have a problem of this nature, you can get information about your state's lemon law at your local library.

You can decrease your chances of getting a lemon by sticking to a vehicle that has a good reputation. I've known people to buy a vehicle that is rated very questionable because they want a specific feature. They get lost in a little picture. Vision gets blurred. They can't see "down the road." Most of these people have a habit of being nearsighted. They can't see problems around the next corner. They can't see the dangers of owning and using an unreliable vehicle.

By buying good vehicles we will be encouraging manufacturers to build better vehicles. Buying habits reflect what goes on the showroom floor. Let's begin by improving our buying habits.

Now, let's take a moment to review the importance of good research. As I've mentioned before, your research into the reliability and values of makes and models of cars, trucks, and RVs should be a pleasurable and challenging experience. To reduce the amount of work, stick to a plan of action. Make changes in the plan at home—not at the dealership. If you want the rewards of a good purchase, do not trust any employee of an auto dealership.

Auto salespeople are trained to manipulate prospects. They are trained to handle every type of buyer. They have seen researchers before. They have tactics to win you over. Good salespeople get their adrenaline flowing by challenging buyers. They love to sharpen their skills on shoppers. If you come across a Smoothy, he will test your limit with effective persuasion. He will challenge you with manipulative techniques that have bilked your friends and relatives of thousands of dollars. He is a professional at what he does.

Your review of the facts at home must be complete. Once you have reviewed the makes and models you are considering, you must review the figures. The figures are critical. You need to know the manufacturer's suggested retail price. You need to know normal discount factors. You need to have a negotiating range. You need to know current interest rates. You need to know payment factors per $100 for each financing term. You need to know the actual cash value of your trade.

Let's see. My car has an ACV of $4,500. Smith wants $13,000 difference before fees so that means I'm paying $17,500 for the car. Browning will sell me one for $16,500 without a trade so that means Smith is only giving me $3,500 for my car. It doesn't seem like Smith is giving me a good deal since my car has a solid wholesale of $4,000. I better see what Browning will do with a trade.

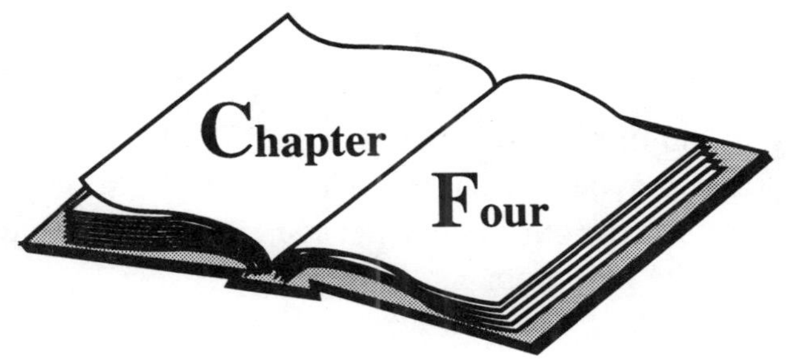

Be Fast On Your Feet

So you think you're ready to go? Well, maybe you are and maybe you aren't. We'll find out soon enough. We'll cross our fingers that a Smoothy won't be waiting for you at the first stop.

Let me stress one final warning before you jump: It'll be easy to take the normal path. Ninety percent of buyers flow with the traffic. Ninety percent of buyers will go with the system whether they trust it or not. Ninety percent of buyers don't think the savings are worth the effort. Ninety percent will never try to break the mold. It's that 90 percent that keeps dealerships rich.

Here we go—ready or not.

You are taking the high road because you are convinced that this vehicle purchase will set trends for your future. You are convinced that what you do now will influence your financial, psychological, and physical welfare for the rest of your life. You will tread carefully because your handling of this purchase will influence how you feel about yourself. You are convinced that this is a test of your mettle. You are convinced that you cannot allow yourself to be led by the nose. You are convinced that a salesperson working on greed should not take an undue amount of your hard-earned money. You are convinced that all auto dealers are manipulators and that a majority of them are bordering on crookedness.

Yes, you are ready to skirmish. You have the most powerful consumer weapons in the world—your fingers and your feet. You cannot lose. The only question is: How much will you win? Before we get into heavy dealing, however, let's review some important points.

You need the salesperson to get you into the system. Regardless what you think of auto salespeople in general, he is most probably just following the rules. The rules of the game have been set by the person who signs his paycheck. The salesperson genuinely wants to make friends as long as it doesn't interfere with making a generous gross profit.

When you are ready to buy, you must indicate to the salesperson that you are a serious buyer. Tell him your timetable. Say, *"I'm willing to buy today, but I do not have to buy today."*

Don't talk payments. Just say that you can buy if the figures are right. Although the salesperson will be reluctant to give you figures without more information, he will do it if you show signs of walking. Since your research is pretty much complete, you know the approximate dealer costs of the vehicle you want. You must *not* tell this to the salesperson.

Your first objective will be to get the salesperson on your side.

The reason you need the salesperson on your side is that you want him to fight for you. He will sense that you won't be a lay-down or an easy-sell, so he needs to taste the commission. If you keep him strung out a bit, he won't turn you prematurely. He'll work hard to keep all the commission and credit to himself.

The way you are received at a dealership will depend on the salesperson's training and personal characteristics. I've seen some of the most successful auto salespeople (constantly earning in the six figures) who never extend a hand. They use a nonchalant approach for the first five minutes—then they begin heavy qualifying. They have their script down so pat that it sounds candid. Their mouths are on autopilot and their brains in high gear. Smoothies don't waste time with tours; they go straight for the throat.

If you meet a Smoothy, you probably won't know it if you're only shopping because he'll dump you fast. Smoothy will be looking for serious buyers because his closing rate—and gross profits—on serious buyers is unbelievably high.

Smoothy is so good he doesn't really need lay-downs, easy-sells, or the system. He's often in trouble with the dealership because he breaks the rules. He's tolerated, however, because he's good at what he does. Thank goodness there aren't too many Smoothies around.

Chances are you'll come face-to-face with a run-of-the-mill salesperson who will try to gain your trust. He or she will be friendly. He or she will probably be someone who you wouldn't mind having for a next-door neighbor. This salesperson will be trained to get you seated so the system can get into high gear. You should consider this seat as the "hot-seat" because a Smoothy will most probably get a shot at you before you leave.

When you know exactly what you want or have a good idea of what you want, you must communicate this to the salesperson and listen to his response. If you've worked with him during the research mode, he'll pretty much know your requirements. He'll know whether you're prone to buying off the inventory, through a factory order, or through a dealer trade. All three require different approaches on his part and different cautions on your part.

The salesperson will want you to buy from stock because it locks up the commission today. Because factory orders require waiting, he can't count on the commission. He knows you can cancel a factory order any time before delivery. His best bet will be to get you excited about something in stock.

A salesperson's second choice will be a dealer trade, but he knows the management hates this process. A dealer trade is time consuming, it's costly, and it obligates the dealer to a competitor. Many managers consider the necessity of a dealer trade as a weakness in the salesperson. "Sell from stock," they'll say.

Whether you buy from inventory, through a dealer trade, or by factory order, you need to lock up the price. You need the

There are big advantages of buying from stock. I can save you money because we have a special sale on right now. The biggest thing, though, is that you don't have to wait. You can drive it home today. Let me show you what I have before you decide.

figures in black and white. You need exact details about what you're getting and what you're paying at the bottom line. Whether the dealer uses a haggle-free or negotiating system, there will be potholes to avoid. The dealership will exert every skill and tactic to get you to bend to its will. You can't let that happen.

We need to talk about an approach that works for some, but does not work for most. The "slam-it-down" approach is quick and dirty. It's fraught with dangers if you don't use it correctly. This approach gives few options to the dealer. The slam-it-down approach is a declaration of war. It allows the dealer to pull all the plugs.

If you walk in and demand a specific price with very little profit, you might find that you've come up against a stone wall. Salespeople get this every day. They know how to work it. They know when the deal is not worth the trouble. If a salesperson is not busy, he may try to convert you into a profit. If he feels you are unreasonable, he will probably drop you like a hot potato. If your offer has an acceptable profit, he will still try for a bump before he takes the offer.

The slam-it-down approach might work well if you know exactly what you want, whether the dealer has it or not, and the dealer cost. You must be willing to walk away if there is one penny variation. I have had some students work this method consistently and successfully because they had all the facts and kept a reasonable profit into the deal for the dealer. This works especially well for busy people who want a quick and clean purchase. This is the only way I recommend any person to approach a system house. To use the slam-it-down approach effectively, you should practice your approach until you have it down pat. It may or may not, however, be for you.

I won't pay one penny beyond this amount.
$13,676

There are those dealers who believe in training the buyers. They make an extra effort to get you and your friends to think payments. They mandate that their salespeople wear suits to get you thinking of them as professional advisors. Their promos push the low prices and good deals because it makes them the "good guys." It's all designed to lead you to the slaughter.

Dealerships have pushed the "make an offer" approach for decades. They're quick to say, "I can understand that you may not be happy with the price, so why not make an offer? The sales manager is pushing for sales today, so you can probably get your price." They want to get you to the desk then turn you, bump you, and make you forget where you started.

If, however, you request a bid from the dealer, the fun and games evaporate. This isn't the way they want it. Bidding is not the game they want to play. Many dealers won't deal with a bid. They'll simply turn it around to, *"Make an offer."*

To get them interested in your offer, you may have to dangle a carrot. When the salesperson asks about financing, it might help if you consider financing with them (more profits). Buying off the inventory might help (today). Being friendly helps (referrals). You promise nothing, but you show flexibility. Turning the tables on an auto dealer isn't hard because he's motivated by greed.

There is a correct way to make an offer, but there are no hard-set rules. Four things, however, must be done before you enter negotiations.

1. You must know exactly what you want to buy. This means that you must separate your search from your buy. You cannot search and buy in one session. Even if the break is for only thirty minutes, there must be a break. Call it a cooling period if you like, but it must exist. It's always best to break with a good night's sleep.

You call me after you think about my offer. I like the truck, but I won't pay what you want.

2. You must know that you can afford the price and the payments. If you find out that the vehicle will not fit into your budget during the negotiations, you must make a

1. **Know exactly what you want.**
2. **Know your budget expenditure and maximum payment you can afford.**
3. **Know the actual cash value of your trade.**
4. **Know where to begin and where to end negotiations.**

break before you continue. Dealers know how to manipulate you into this position, how to bump when you are most vulnerable, and how to extract every penny financing will allow.

3. You must know the actual cash value (ACV) of your trade. You cannot negotiate a close deal unless you know the ACV of your trade. Dealers know how to bump you on the trade. They have tricks to convince you why your trade is worth less than you think. You must think of the difference between what you owe and the trade's actual cash value as real cash that you're putting on the desk.

4. You must know at what figure you will begin and at what figure you will walk away. These figures cannot be compromised once you enter the dealership. If compromising enters the picture, you must take a break to redo your calculations.

There is always the salesperson who can't seem to get down to business. The ““wear-'em-out” technique involves heavy qualifying and extensive inventory tours. Sometimes it works. I have seen buyers so worn out that they actually give up and buy. Don't let this happen to you. Set a time limit. If the tour and presentation appear to be dragging out, give a hint that you have to be leaving. The salesperson will then try to get you to the desk to make his pitch for the sale today. If you are still in your research mode, make it clear that you are not ready to buy today. If, however, you indicate that you are ready to buy, he will immediately get into a negotiating gear. This is where you want him. When he mentions "offer" you can use your beginning figure. You know where to begin and where to walk.

I'm sorry to take so long, but we're so close to what you want that the sales manager would like to work it out with you himself.

There is nothing like a hint of walking to get the salesperson talking seriously. If, however, he feels he is stopped, he will turn you to another salesperson (always with an impressive title) or to a sales manager. If the new entry tries to start the whole process again, give him a quick refresher from your notes. Allow up to 15 minutes then begin to get fidgety. Do not respond to his questions. Stand up. If he asks you to sit down again, you might have him going your way; so give him another few minutes. Do not accept coffee or soft drink. Keep talk to a minimum.

You must be ready to walk, sneak away, or flat-out run. Do whatever you have to do to get away if things get too hot. Dealers know how to cook buyers.

You will probably walk away from one or two dealerships before you decide to move up from your bottom line. Don't do it too soon. Recently, I had a student firm everything up at one dealership then get more options and a better price at another dealership. He told them outright that he had a deposit somewhere else. Although the only car they had to match was well equipped, he still wanted a $300 better deal. He got the better car and the better price. He got it because they knew they had one shot. They were willing to make a slim profit to steal a sale from another dealer. That's the way it works.

It's true that a deal today may not be a deal tomorrow, but chances are it will be. If, however, you put forth an offer that is accepted, you must follow through with a good-faith deposit—which is never more than a couple of hundred dollars. If you get a better offer the next morning, you can cancel the

If you can't sneak away,

you can always flat-out run.

deal or renegotiate. The rules of the road are for all the players. Until you sign the final papers and drive off the sales lot, you do not own the vehicle.

I have known buyers who walk away a number of times before they get what they want. They start to walk and are stopped in the building. They walk again and are stopped

outside the door. They walk again and are stopped after they start the engine. Some salespeople are experts at watching prospects walk away. They know when to stop them and how to bring them back. They play a good game.

An auto dealer is always ready to replace any salesperson who doesn't perform. Knowing this can put you in the driver's seat as soon as you sit at the desk. You can lay it on the line by saying, "I'd like to buy this car from you, so that you can get <u>all</u> the credit for the sale. If we can work it out, I can help you make more sales." A statement like this gets the salesperson working for you because no salesperson wants to split a commission. Even in a haggle-free dealership there is some incentive involved. There are many ways for an auto dealer to increase the gross profit—such as taking a trade below book value, pushing dealer add-ons, and making large profits in the back-end.

Neophyte salespeople will be on the first line. Beginners are watched closely by the management. Don't, however, go for the line, *"I'm new here, so I'm willing to work harder for you."* This line is often used by the most experienced Smoothies. Don't modify your strategy because you want to help a beginner. This is a trap.

Don't waste your time with salespeople who beat around the bush. By showing signs of walking you will probably get someone better. If you get turned directly to a closer, you can expect professional treatment. You must understand, however, that the closer is the best salesperson the dealer has—possibly a Smoothy. You'll be given the hard sell. You'll get pressure. Expect it. Be friendly and hold the line. You'll easily save $200 to $1,000 by playing the game. If it doesn't work, go back another day.

Turning you to another salesperson is the real test of your resolve. Most salespeople will turn you when they're stopped but think a deal is still possible. You probably won't get turned, however, if you're so firm that the sales manager doesn't want to bother with you.

Being turned doesn't mean that you're too low. Sometimes the salesperson will turn you to a closer even if the deal is good as it stands. I know of a used truck deal that had a $3,000 profit before it was bumped for an additional $1,000. That bump took exactly five minutes after a turn.

Sometimes the turn is designed to get you into another environment. If you are turned to the sales manager's plush office, watch out. This is usually what happens to lay-downs. The dealer has a good deal going. It's been easy. Why not go for broke?

The closer will tell you how badly he wants your business. He will explain that the dealer must make a reasonable profit to keep the doors open. *"We want to give you good service and attention,"* he will say, *"but we can't do that without making some profit."* (The bleeding heart technique.) *"We are willing to compromise, however, if you can give a little. Let's both be fair."* (Ho, ho, ho!)

When you start getting the stories, keep your face neutral and stiffen your body. Cross your arms. The closer will be watching you for body signs. Don't frown or smile. Keep a poker face. When he gets to the compromise, simply shake your head and stand up. It's time to walk.

Every dealer has a worksheet that the salesperson uses to manipulate the buyer. When he brings out the worksheet, give him basic information but do not give your Social Security number. You do not want a credit check at this time. By giving name, address, and telephone number you are showing that you are willing to buy today or that he can contact you later. You are giving him a tool but not the toolbox.

As the worksheet bounces between the salesperson and the sales manager, it will get modified with colored scribbling. Your own notes must reflect the true results of the skirmishing. Believe me, it's all a big game to build profit into the deal. It's a game to test your resolve.

If you are with someone, do not talk about the deal when left alone. Many closing offices are bugged. Illegal though it is, it happens. Relax, take deep breaths, and be patient. You have the winning ingredients: your feet and you fingers.

In some dealerships, there are three levels to keep you

from getting away. You might have to go through the salesperson, a closer, and a sales manager before you can find out if they'll take your offer. If you give a little on the first round, they will expect that you'll give more on the second round. That's okay.

The second round is most important. Probably you will get your deal here. If you are friendly but firm, they'll begin to move in your direction. If you find the deal is staying too close to your maximum limit, it will be time to fly away—a time of decision.

Give me $50 more and I'll take the deal.
I'll throw in the undercoating!
How about splitting the difference?

If you get the deal you want, it isn't over yet. There's still the matter of payment and of being sure you get the vehicle you bargained for. The dealer has plans of making more profit on the deal than you left with the closer.

If you are a payment buyer, the salesperson will work hard to keep the payment figure more in focus than the vehicle price. He will be vague about interest rates and terms until the deal gets closed. If you push hard on payments, they might give you these figures immediately. Be careful, however, they have ways of misleading you—which I'll illustrate in the next chapter.

Through manufacturer financing, auto dealers can sometimes give better financing on new vehicles than banks and credit unions. They use this to push new car purchases and sell extended warranties. They always get big incentives for financing. Auto dealers never give it away. They always make profit.

Your prospect wants what figures?

Don't let the closer work you on payment figures. Be sure you get the interest rate and term every time you get new figures. It must always include four figures: 1) amount financed, 2) interest rate, 3) term, and 4) payment. Remember! That's four figures. They'll try to confuse you on the issue

If you get confused about any part of the deal, leave a small deposit to lock up the purchase price only and go home. You have their figures. They won't like it, but they'll go along with it. Don't leave your trade—bring it back tomorrow. The deal isn't done yet. You can still get caught.

The dealer is not your friend. If you buy from him, you will be his customer. It will never be more than that. You'll exist on his computers as a money-making entity. You are nothing more than a name with a history of giving him profits. You are an asset on the dealer's books. That's how the system works.

Sometimes you can get particulars about the dealer by developing friendships with the regular employees. These associations can give you answers to important questions and possibly get you preferential treatment when you get ready to deal.

It doesn't work the same way with salespeople. Salespeople work on commission and are controlled by the system. Being the friend of a salesperson may help you get a minimum deal a little quicker, but smart buyers usually do better with a stranger.

Auto salespeople can be quick to call a prospect a “flake” (meaning: a nothing) if he doesn't buy. They can tear, rip, and destroy at will. I've seen auto salespeople who've had a bad month purposely lay little old ladies away. I've seen salespeople give wonderful people the finger because they weren't lay-downs. I know of a successful RV salesperson who habitually treats customers like gold before they buy—and like dung after they buy.

Almost every salesperson will be nice to your face. Some will be genuine in their desire to help you. Most will estimate the profits, however, before they give you much time. Don't lose sleep because you can't work a deal with a “friendly” salesperson.

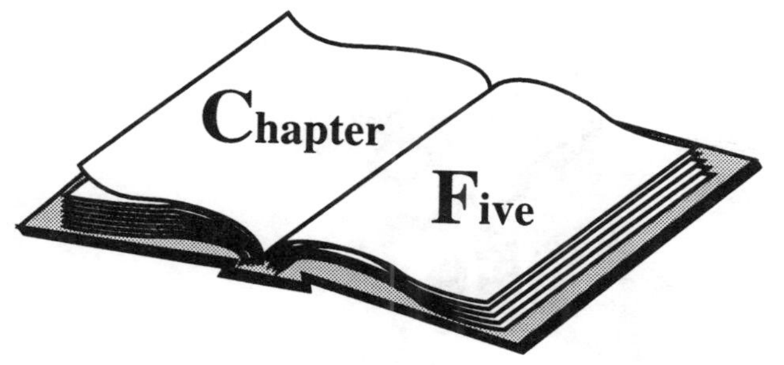

Beware of the Back-end

You made the deal! You're satisfied that you made a good deal because you got what you wanted at $460 over invoice. You're excited because you've worked hard to get to this point. You've done the proper research and leg work. But before you go home, you have to sign some papers. You are scheduled for the back-end.

Good deals turn sour all the time. People make good deals then rush into the business office. They come face-to-face with a very proficient finance officer who's going to get them on the road in just a few minutes. Many buyers have never figured out that the business office is part of the system to rip them off. Some get caught for thousands of dollars.

As you celebrate your purchase, our back-end expert (I call him or her BEE) is watching. BEE is studying the deal and your profile. BEE already knows much about you because he worked the financing. Because BEE is paid on an incentive basis, he has to make a profit before he gets paid.

There are as many dirty tricks played on auto consumers in the back-end as on the sales lot. You need to prepare yourself for your visit to the business office because you'll be coming face-to-face with an expert persuader.

When the taste of victory is on your lips, you can easily say, "Yes!" If you do, you will lose. You may be better prepared than most, but you do not have the experience of that person whose job is to stick it to you in the back-end.

I realize, Mike, that the payment will take them close to forty percent debt-to-income, but Bill's going to get a raise soon and Mary will be getting back to work in a couple of months. These are straight, mature people. You owe me for the last six good ones I sent you.

BEE knows all about you. He or she was instrumental in getting your financing approved or, at the very least, BEE's been studying the deal. BEE's even trained the salesperson to get you primed for the back-end pitch. In many dealerships the salesperson gets a bonus if back-end efforts are successful.

BEE is not unlike the dessert girl in the fancy restaurant who tries to entice you into wonderful pies, cakes, and puddings. BEE expects you to have an inclination to say "No!" to her pitch for an extended service agreement, payment protection insurance, and auto protective coatings. But because profits are big in this department, BEE's chair is reserved for the best salesperson the dealer can find.

BEE begins by working the financing institution to get the most profit from the deal. BEE knows every angle to get your financing approved. BEE has tricks to be tried even if your credit isn't that good. The loan officer at the bank may smell a rotting fish, but he may still approve the loan. He may suspect that the interest will be far above the buy-rate, but he may shrug and let it ride. He could suspect that the purchased

Let's see. He' s a bookkeeper retiring in about seven years. Only a few thousand in the bank. She's never worked. Perfect for insurance and extended warranty.

vehicle or trade-in is over-evaluated, but he may still buy the deal.

Banks make money on loans. The bigger the dealership, the more they'll give in to the demands of the dealer. BEE will work the bank because the dealership makes money on interest. BEE knows that if she can handle the financing, she will have a better chance of getting you to say "Yes" to her pitches. BEE knows that the easiest task will be to sell you once you get into her office. She's done it so many times that it's automatic. Now that you think you have a good deal on the car, she will lay you away in the back-end. She'll work the payment protection into the deal so smoothly that you might not even realize it's there. She'll be so smooth on the extended warranty that you'll feel like saying "please." BEE goes beyond being cunning—BEE is smart.

BEE has had plenty of time to study you. After you've completed the purchase, you might even have to wait a few minutes for BEE to get her strategy worked out. A lot of profit depends upon her preparation.

BEE might be called the F & I officer (finance and insurance), finance manager, or the business manager. Regardless of his or her title, you can bet that she makes between $50,000 and $100,000 every year. I've known BEEs to make as much as $20,000 in commissions in one month. That's one month! They make this much because profits in the back-end are phenomenally high.

BEE is a professional. She is a department in herself. She handles the customers of at least 10 salespeople. She has to make more profit without losing the deal as it stands. Most BEEs are experts.

Now that you have an idea that BEE is something other than a clerk in the back office, you probably think you're well prepared. But don't be so sure. BEE is almost perfectly designed for getting you to switch from any preconceived ideas.

BEE is a music maker. Everything he or she says will be tuned with a beat to get your emotions high. His lyrics will fit the mood, and he'll have them down pat. From the moment you step into his office, he'll have one objective—to get you dancing to his tune.

Time and time again I'm going to tell you that BEE is a Smoothy of Smoothies. If you forget it for one moment, he'll take money from your pocket. His pitch is perfect. He knows how to waltz and how to rap.

Now and then buyers come across a BEE who's a trainee. Trainees are taught to get you on their side. They'll invoke sympathy. The system is designed to cover training. Even if the music is slightly off beat, the message will be the same.

Keep in mind that BEE is a maestro at what he does. From greeting to leaving, he will hold the baton. If you don't like his tune for payment protection, he will switch into a song about coverage on those expensive repairs after the standard warranty runs out.

You'd think that BEE would be afraid to talk about his product falling apart, but he won't be. He plays the tune so well that you won't even question him on the reliability of the vehicle. You'll just want to be sure that you aren't caught unprotected. He can even cover you on payments for this protection. It's a "pay-as-you-go program." It's so easy. "Just initial in this box," he says, "and you'll be covered."

BEE can be very sweet. He can be the father type or the grandfather type. She can be the mother type or the grandmother type. BEE has been known to have an inventory of pictures to decorate his desk after studying the prospect's profile. BEE knows how and when to push on fear. BEE knows how to work on conscience. BEE always shows concern for you—as long as you're receptive.

When I went to F & I (finance and insurance) school, I constantly marveled at those who were there for a refresher course. During the role play the women, in particular, had words and phrases that could turn a Scrooge into a saint. They demonstrated some of the manipulative ways to overcome objections. The power of words combined with a motherly stature was marvelous to behold.

Oh yes, I remember the advice I gave to my wonderful children.

Although I know what BEE will be saying, I can't claim that his statements will be stale. There is nothing stale about BEE's words. Everything he or she says will sound candid and honest. Everything said will be natural. A good BEE is a wolf in cuddly lamb's clothing. It all works like magic. The magician casts a spell, moves the magic wand, and you believe. If you nod just once, the spell will hold.

Try to think of yourself as an auto dealer who relies on back-end sales to keep his doors open. Who would you hire as a back-end expert? I'm sure you'd hire the smoothest persuader you could find. You can bet that the BEE you'll be meeting will be that person.

In smaller auto and RV dealerships, back-end services are often sold by the salesperson or the sales manager. This could

make it somewhat easier on the buyer because those involved in the vehicle sale won't jeopardize the primary sale by applying too much pressure. If you say, "No!" under such a scenario, the subject should be dropped.

In big or small dealerships, the big money is made through financing. If BEE can get you approved at 10 percent and his buy-rate is 6 percent, the dealership will realize a profit of 40 percent of every dollar you pay in interest. All you need to do is look at the financing contract—it's easy to figure.

Since auto dealers usually get a buy-rate slightly below the lowest interest rate charged by major credit unions, a little checking will give you an approximate buy-rate. You'll see why dealers can often match credit unions and very often beat the banks' regular rate. You'll see why they can easily finance you with an interest rate somewhere between the credit union rate and the bank rate and still make a profit.

Before you go into BEE's office, you should know what to expect in an interest rate. You should also know the term (duration of the loan in months) and any special requirements. You cannot rely on the salesperson to help you. You cannot rely on BEE to tell you the truth. There's a long history of abuses heaped upon buyers after the deal has been negotiated. The business office can be your Waterloo. If you have not prepared properly, you will probably lose. Now that you have an idea of what to expect, let's go through the process and try to outwit BEE.

BEE's greeting will usually bowl you over. As a professional, BEE knows that the seeds of trust are sown at the greeting. BEE knows that prospects must be greeted according to their profile. If he's had to work hard to get your financing approved, he will be friendly but very businesslike and slightly aloof. If he's greeting a retired couple, he'll relax them with a bit of small-talk. He'll be a chameleon—changing colors to camouflage his real purpose.

You should expect BEE to get right down to business. You don't have time for games. Say as little as possible. By folding your arms across your chest you'll be indicating that you're going to resist a sales pitch. You've nothing to gain by being friendly to BEE. The purchase is in the bag. You want straight facts about financing and registration—that's all.

You should not expect to say "Yes" to any of BEE's sales pitches. If, however, you have questions about payment protection, repair protection, or coatings, keep them brief. You must always remember that BEE has met your type many times before.

BEE is human. By showing resistance, you will be lowering his expectations and possibly his resolve. If you indicate right away that you're in his office only for financing and registration (or payment-in-full and registration), he might write you off early to get on to the next prospect.

Expect anything from BEE. As I've warned, BEE is a professional salesperson who eats buyers like you'd eat candy. He's never easy. Once you get behind the desk, you will find that BEE is truly an expert. He will be friendly one moment and serious the next. He'll tie the friendliness and the seriousness together because he's concerned for your future. You'll find that BEE knows how to conjure up the right visions as he tries to sell you payment protection. He knows how to be firm at the right time. He knows how to get to your conscience—and your checkbook.

I wouldn't sell you anything I didn't believe in myself. My new car is fully undercoated, has the Gold Coat 10-year polish, and my children can spill anything on the seats without leaving stains. I can assure you that my car will look like new when I trade it in five years. And I'll get the highest trade-in allowance possible.

You may buy ten vehicles in a lifetime, but BEE works with that many buyers in one day. You are not an expert buyer, but BEE is an expert seller. You, however, do not need to be an expert in BEE's office because you are in charge. Without your signature BEE gets nothing. You can stop the process at any time and walk away. That is BEE's nightmare.

When BEE starts selling you payment insurance, hold a hand in front of your head, palm facing BEE, and say, "I don't want it." Don't let the discussion go any further.

If, however, you have serious health problems and there are no restrictions on the insurance, you might want to consider the simplest program. If such a scenario exists, let him quote his price for simple term and then say, "It's too much. Reduce it by 20 percent and I'll look it over." You can bet BEE's still making 30 percent for the dealership. If you question the value, just say, "No!"

Since you know you will be approached on the subject, call your local insurance agent and get the going rates for decreasing term insurance. It'll pay.

BEE will also be good at selling you an extended service agreement. He'll have ways of convincing you that an extended warranty or a service agreement will probably save you money. He'll also tell you about the security that goes with such a protection package. BEE will not tell you, of course, that you'll probably collect less than 25 percent of what you'll pay for the service. He also won't tell you the total cost of the service—which will be financed at the regular rate.

Let's suppose that BEE gets you a payment of $287 per month at an attractive interest rate. He tells you all the features of the extended service agreement, but you remain unconvinced. BEE obviously feels you should have this protection program. You're beginning to think positive, but can't quite say "Yes."

"I understand your hesitation to increase the payment," BEE says, "but if I can work it so that your payment is not increased by one penny, would you be interested?"

If you say, "No!," he'll go on until he gets a "Yes." So, we'll assume you say, "Yes."

Now BEE will work at his computer for a minute or so and then look at you, smile, and say, "I've done it! I can get you the entire program for $284 a month. That's $3 less than I thought I could do."

You say, "Yes," and you're caught by one of BEE's tricks. All he did was increase the term by one year—something he'd have done anyway to get more interest profits. You've been had.

BEE won't hesitate to talk about the body and interior protection packages that she claims will make the car an investment. She'll know how to use the right words and phrases because she's done it hundreds of times before. And, of course, BEE has a good incentive. She'll be getting a good commission from the very high gross profit that the dealer will realize. She might even believe some of what she's saying because good salespeople believe in their products.

The profits in both exterior and interior protective coatings are phenomenal. I've seen minimum-wage workers spend three hours on a $250 polish job. Including finance charges (more profit), the total cost could easily reach $400. Interior protection packages bring even more profit. Undercoating done at a dealership is generally overpriced and low in quality.

BEE knows that you're hot to protect your new vehicle. If you have young children, BEE will assume you want the protection. "Kids are rough on the interior," he or she will say. "By keeping the upholstery like new you'll get a much better allowance when you trade it in five or seven years. This inexpensive protection will be one of the best investments you'll ever make." With these wonderful sounding words you'll soon forget the extra $10 in monthly payments for the 50 or 60 months. BEE will have lots of ammunition in his arsenal.

Of course, if you leave BEE in an unhappy mood, that's all right too. You have to look after yourself for the rest of your life. BEE won't be there when the refrigerator gets empty. He won't be there if you want to change cars but owe too much on it to do so. You'll find BEE does a good job of taking care of BEE. You must say, "I must take care of me."

After taking many calls and doing many analytical interviews, it is still surprising to me how many otherwise smart buyers think BEE deserves a tip. They say, "No!, No!, No!,"

Mechanics, of course, like this upward spiral in electronic equipment because they can charge $60 an hour for repairs. Although electronic devices generally work very well, the cost of repairs can be a shocker. Our extended service agreement will eliminate that shock and protect your budget.

Fiction!

Fact!

It says here that the car's computer won't be covered unless we have the wheel bearings packed every 40,000 miles—which we have to pay for.

then "Okay." It's like telling me that they felt BEE deserved something for all his work. They tip him with a small payment protection plan, or a lesser extended service agreement, or undercoating. Let's face it: BEE won!

BEE usually accomplishes exactly what the system wants him to accomplish. He doesn't always get it all, but he usually gets something. BEE doesn't deserve anything. His office should be a business cost. Whatever profits the dealership makes from the sale of the vehicle should absorb the expense of the back-end. To make so much profit in the back-end is to mislead the public. It adds up to a big con game.

Don't feel bad about refusing to give BEE anything. He will automatically make a few hundred dollars if he handles the financing. If he doesn't get the financing, that's okay too. Take your good deal and run. Don't look back to see if BEE is unhappy or not. It really doesn't matter.

We said "No!" and he wasn't even upset.

Now that you've left BEE's office and are safe and snug at home, take a few minutes and review the events and the paperwork. It's the best time to prepare for your next purchase—and another meeting with BEE.

If you bought something from BEE, you have probably been tricked in one way or another. You might find that your scanning of the contract didn't seem so important because BEE called it an "agreement" or maybe just "paperwork."

You might find that the figures aren't exactly as you expected them. You might find everything in order but the outcome wasn't exactly what you wanted when you went in. BEE knows how to get things his way.

When you do get down to needing the services you were sold by BEE, you might find that they aren't exactly what you expected. You might find that you rushed through the small print in BEE's office.

You probably once thought that BEE earns a reasonable salary with a bonus. Now you know better. If you feel good about the services you bought from BEE, that's perfectly okay. If, however, you feel that you were persuaded into getting something you didn't need, you can count it as a learning experience. Think about it for a few minutes, then put it away. Of course, BEE will never remember you when you have financial troubles or if the car breaks down. It's out of his hands now. You signed the papers. You authorized him to act in your behalf. You gave him your confidence because he was a nice guy. You are now only an entry in the computer.

In this chapter I've tried to impress you with the importance of preparing for the back-end. I have done this because 90 percent of buyers leave money with BEE that they didn't want to leave. Auto, truck, and RV salespeople support back-end experts with all types of tricks to get you to do what your gut feeling says you shouldn't do. They use your emotions to their benefit. They are experts at chopping away at your resolve. They know how to twist to get more than a reasonable profit.

Now that you know what happens in the business office, you should never get stung by BEE. Keep in mind that whatever BEE sells you will cost you twice as much over the life of the car. An extended service agreement doesn't cost you $800—it'll cost you at least $1,300 when you include the interest. Thirteen hundred dollars pays for a lot of repairs. Protective coatings can be applied better and cheaper elsewhere. Don't finance these services.

If you're not sure how you should react to BEE's pitch, why not just say, "No!" If you say "No!" you'll be almost sure of doing the right thing. By saying "No!" you will feel good about yourself. By saying "No!" you will keep the good deal you're going to make on the car. After all, the reason you're doing all of this study is to get a good deal.

With the knowledge you've acquired from this book, you can easily outwit any auto, truck, or RV dealer—and you can do it every time. By saying "No" and using your feet for a fast exit, you have the ultimate weapon against Smoothy. If you're retired, you'll save enough to expand your wonderful retirement activities. If you're still working, you'll be saving enough to make your retirement more secure. If you're just beginning to build your financial future, you'll be getting into a habit that will put you in the top ten percent of people who are financially secure.

You should, regardless of your current status, use many of these buying principles in other types of purchases. When you develop an attitude and philosophy of controlling your spending, you'll not only feel like a better person, you will be a better person.

Now, go to the Glossary and learn more!

jd gallant

A Glossary of Terms You *Must* Know

ACV:

ACV is the actual cash value of the vehicle. It is the most important thing to know if you want to avoid being manipulated when trading a vehicle or buying a used vehicle. It represents true cash. It is what you can readily get for it from a dealer or at an auction. It is *not* trade-in allowance. It is *not* fair-market value. It is *not* retail. It is the actual cash value to a dealer who plans on retailing it.

The ACV of a vehicle will change from dealer to dealer. Like chocolate, a specific model could be poison to one and dessert to another. I consider ACV as an average of five local sources. This might include two appraisal book figures and three bids from used car dealers. (Because new car dealers usually auction or wholesale many of their trade-ins, they buy much lower than wholesale.) Since some used car dealers always try to "steal" private-party vehicles, I avoid any bid more than 20 percent below average appraisal book. If your vehicle is older than what the dealer normally sells, his ACV on your vehicle will be below wholesale. In such a scenario, you are almost always better off selling the vehicle on your own.

The ACV at every dealership should be close to the N.A.D.A. Appraisal Guide or Kelley Blue Book wholesale, plus optional equipment, plus or minus mileage, plus or minus condition, plus or minus the dealership's desire to own it. If your vehicle is average, the ACV should be within 10 percent of the book appraisal. You must keep in mind, however, that many dealerships use both the Kelley Blue Book and the N.A.D.A. book. They will try to buy at the lowest figure and sell at the highest figure. RV Consumer Group uses an average appraisal book figure that represents a true ACV for RVs.

add-ons:

Dealers can add whatever they want to a supplementary

price sheet. They can charge whatever price they want. They can install a $29 stereo and charge you $295 for it. They can charge preparation. They can charge $150 for a $10 polish job. They always triple their cost on pin-striping. They can add whatever they want to the supplementary price sheet as long as they have the MSRP (manufacturer's suggested retail price) sheet attached to the window to new cars and trucks.

advertised price:

If you find that a vehicle you've made a deposit on has an advertised price lower than that of your contract, you probably have good recourse for an adjustment. I have seen many cases where a dealer sells a specific auto, truck, or RV for a much higher price than that advertised in a local paper. Check those advertisements before and after the deal is made. Once you sign registration papers and take the vehicle home, however, it's generally too late for an adjustment.

appraisal:

Always be present during an appraisal and appraisal drive. Get your keys back immediately after the drive. There is a long list of tricks to use against those who are generous with trade-in keys.

A salesperson is very careful not to offend you when appraising your vehicle, but a good appraiser will let you know that it has blemishes and wear. Don't let him diminish the value with frowns and touches to body flaws. If he revs the engine, you must frown to let him know that you care about *your* car—which you *might* keep.

appraisal book:

Kelley Blue Book and N.A.D.A produce the most commonly used appraisal books for autos, trucks, RV, boats, aircraft, and mobile homes. These appraisal books give wholesale, retail, and original (base) MSRP. Some books have a column for average trade-in. The only figure that is of any value to the smart buyer, however, is the wholesale figure. If the wholesale figure is not listed, you'll find a loan value column that represents the wholesale figure. Appraisal books are made for the auto salesperson—not the consumer .

Keep in mind that all appraisal books are strictly guides. If a salesperson shows you a figure in any appraisal book, take the book from his hand and study it. They love to flash those small figures at you then throw the book back into the desk drawer. Pay no mind, it's only more trickery.

Appraisal books are usually available at public libraries.

APR:

APR is the annual percentage rate. It reflects all loan costs. Federal law requires that the APR is written on your contract. The trick of the salesperson or BEE is to get you thinking simple interest because it is usually lower. Don't think simple. Ask for the APR: annual percentage rate.

as-is:

Buy "as-is" cars, trucks, and RVs below the book price. If there is no warranty given on the vehicle, you need to know why. Some states may require the posting—but find out before you buy it. There is nothing wrong with buying a used vehicle without a warranty providing you know the fair-market price and the risk you're taking. (See "back of book.")

asking price:

When you go shopping for a new car or truck you will be dealing with five figures: 1) the posted price, 2) the manufacturer's suggested retail price (MSRP), 3) the bottom price, 4) the invoice, and 5) below invoice profit. Somewhere in there you'll find an asking price—a figure that will change from salesperson to salesperson and moment to moment. Your objective will be to skirt the asking price and the MSRP to get down to the bottom price.

auto-salesperson profile:

The profile that most people have of a typical car salesperson is that of a smooth talker, an aggressive seller, and a big spender. A smart auto salesperson will try to shatter this aura by being super friendly and helpful. If he can get you thinking how he is an exception to the auto-salesperson profile, his deception will have worked. Keep in mind that almost everyone who buys a vehicle thinks they have a good deal and that their salesperson was "nice." If it weren't so, they wouldn't have made the purchase.

Don't go by what your friends and relatives say about the deal they got. Don't trust any salesperson because someone else says, "He's okay."

Bonuses are offered to salespeople for performance. These bonuses usually terminate at the end of the week or at the end of the month. At these times, salespeople will be aggressive to a point of desperation.

Weekends are usually busy. Every salesperson will be anxious to sell a number of vehicles on Saturdays and Sundays. If you know what you want and show that you're a "today" buyer, he'll want to get you in and out in a hurry. He can't afford to have you cluttering his office while "hot" buyers are all over the place. If it's not a turnover house, the salesperson won't turn you to another unless you get him against the wall. Your goal will be to let him know right away that you'll buy with the right deal. Keep telling him this as you stay within the figures on your notepad. When he tries to confuse the issue, simply ask him if he wants your business. If he starts to hem and haw, it'll be time to stand up as if you're going to leave. At this point he'll resolve something fast or

turn you to a sales manager. Because auto and RV salespeople rely on weekend sales to make their quotas, well informed and disciplined buyers can work weekends to their advantage.

In both autos and RVs the salesperson usually gets a minimum commission if the house accepts the deal regardless of the profit. If, for example, the dealership accepts an invoice deal, the salesperson still makes something for his time plus he'll get a number towards a volume bonus. Never feel sorry for an auto or RV salesperson—the good ones probably make more money than you do.

back-end:

As much as I preach against letting the guard down once the price is satisfactorily negotiated, most buyers still get caught in the back-end. If you cannot give a resounding "No!" immediately after the back-end expert gives you the sales pitch, there is little chance for you to get away unscathed.

The back-end expert (I call him or her BEE.) is usually called the F&I manager (finance and insurance), the finance officer, or the business manager. Regardless what he is called, BEE is always a smooth salesperson. A current report on earnings within the auto industry showed that the average annual income of a back-end expert was almost $100,000. With that as an average, you can imagine what a queen BEE could be earning.

BEE's salary is usually all commission. I have met many BEEs who could not sell in a normal sales situation but are making big bucks simply by learning a pitch that works and sticking to it. The profits and commissions on back-end services such as life insurance, disability insurance, extended warranties, and after-sale optional services would make P. T. Barnum envious.

A training seminar that I attended for F&I managers was a learning experience. As I type these words, I have the seminar's training manual in front of me. The techniques illustrated are proven to work. The manual explains in detail how to greet, how to analyze, how to present, how to overcome objections, and how to put on the pressure. It explains in detail how to respond to a specific remark or question. It points out that although 67 percent of new-car buyers dislike the F&I experience, in most auto dealerships the profits from the F&I department are equal to, or exceed, the profits of the sales department.

Now I must admit that everything about the back-end isn't bad. Some of the services might be worth hearing about and possibly considering. The service itself may not necessarily be bad, but the price almost always is.

back of book:

When a vehicle make or model has something undesirable about it, it will have a wholesale and retail value below the book value. "Twenty percent back of book" would mean that you will deduct 20 percent from both values. Back of book is not the same as a deduction for condition or mileage. A make or model that is known to be seriously flawed is always purchased or traded back of book.

balance sheet:

If a salesperson whips out a blank piece of paper, draws a line down the middle, and proceeds to help you make a decision between models, you have encountered the balance sheet close. If you need that kind of help, go home and start over.

bid:

Dealers hate to make a bid to a consumer. Many dealers won't make a bid to anyone except commercial accounts. If you tell a dealer you want their lowest price because you'll buy where you get the best deal, you're actually asking them to bid for your business. A smart dealer will not get caught up in this game. It's bad for the entire industry because it opens up a big can of worms.

When you use the bid approach, you'll probably never get an official bid anyway. A smart salesperson will work you to find out how firm you are. He'll use years of experience to break you down and wear you out. He'll first try to switch you from the "bid" to an "offer." If you're too hard, he might write a number on his card and let you go. Unless you know exactly what you're doing, that number means nothing.

bird-dog:

A bird-dog is a person who sends another person to a particular salesperson to buy a vehicle. Bird-dog fees are paid in cash after the deal is consummated. Mechanics are often enlisted as bird-dogs. Some very successful salespeople mention this "bonus" to every person to whom they sell a vehicle.

Because bird-dogs are common in the auto sales arena, you have to be very careful about using a recommendation for a particular salesperson.

bottom price:

"I want the bottom price," is a statement every salesperson hears every day. It means nothing in the real world of auto dealing.

Unless you get involved with buying services such as RV Consumer Group or Consumer Reports, hard negotiating is the only way to get to the bottom price. When you find the exact vehicle for you, whether new or used, you must be ready to negotiate. To negotiate well, you need the facts. Even if you go to a "haggle-free" dealership, you still will have to deal somewhere along the line. Get the facts then go for the bottom price.

brand:

Most auto, truck, and RV manufacturers produce more than one brand or make. In autos and trucks, we usually refer to them as makes, whereas in RVs we refer to them as brands. These names are usually illustrated larger than the manufacturer's name or logo.

broker:

Buying through an automobile broker has few advantages and many disadvantages. The broker carries no stock and must order through a system that requires a fee in addition to the price of the vehicle. If you road test at a dealership with plans to buy from a broker, you are actually stealing from the dealership. Many brokers will do all the tricks that a dealer will do. When buying new, it is usually best to avoid the broker. Learn to work with dealerships the right way and you'll be better off. Buying an RV through a well-known broker, however, can have some advantages. Some brokers can accumulate hundreds of RVs in an up-to-date computerized inventory list. Because buying an RV requires an extensive knowledge of the manufacturer, brand, and model, it is always best to check out the RV and the broker through RV Consumer Group.

bugs:

Although not legal, "bugging" a closing room is not unheard of. Eavesdropping is quite common. Do not talk about the deal when the salesperson leaves to consult with the sales manager. The walls are thin! If appropriate, you can hold hands, write notes, whisper, wink, or kiss, but don't talk about the deal.

carryovers:

Carryovers are stock in inventory when new models are

available. Generally carryovers can be purchased at or below invoice only *after* the new models are fully stocked. By this time, not much choice is available. This is a time to watch out for a "bait and switch" or other tricks. Carryovers can be a good buy if you are flexible on options and colors.

When dealing, consider that carryovers will usually have a dealer rebate (not a consumer rebate) of about 5 percent of the invoice. If you add this rebate to the hold-back that the dealer gets, it should be clear that buying a carryover below invoice is quite possible. By dealing hard, you might find yourself with a good deal with minimum effort.

Because carryovers make sense, salespeople use them to their advantage. Most carryovers are sold well above invoice to make the dealer very high profits. (See "hold-back.")

contract:

You'll never hear the word "contract" from a good salesperson. It'll be "paperwork" or "agreement." Regardless what the salesperson or F&I officer calls it, it's a binding contract when you sign it and services have been exchanged.

When you are at the desk, always keep in mind that whatever the salesperson says is never binding; but what you say is always binding. This condition is real. It has permeated the American buying psyche to an extent that it is difficult to break the mold. As an example, you say, "Sure, I'll buy it for $14,250," and you'll feel obligated. If the salesperson says, "Sure, I can get it for you at that price," you don't really believe it and he doesn't consider it dishonest. I can't tell you how to build a personal buying philosophy, but you should never feel dishonest about changing your mind when dealing with an auto dealership. If the goose can do it, the gander can do it.

The biggest trick is changing figures on the contract from that agreed upon. Most buyers will not catch these subtle changes because they are eager to get away with their new vehicle. The salesperson, closer, or F&I officer have many ways of distracting you. They'll compliment you, talk about the weather, and do just about anything to keep your mind occupied. They'll work hard to confuse you. They'll cover figures with the hand to hold the paper down, pass you the pen with a distracting remark, or do something dramatic if you study it too closely. I cannot emphasize enough that you hold the papers in your hands and take at least five minutes to study the figures and print. Always use a calculator.

You also need to watch out for implied contracts. They are often as binding as a signed contract. A dealer may stick a buyer with an implied contract by letting the buyer use the car for a number of days. If the buyer uses it as if he owns it, he could be stuck with it. It will depend on the judge, but it has happened and it will continue to happen.

Do not take a vehicle for extended use under any condition. If the salesperson says, "Go ahead, use it for a few days," don't think he's being kind. He's got nothing on his mind except sticking you with the vehicle. In the meantime, he'll sell or auction your trade-in and you're really stuck.

cooling-off period:

Cooling-off periods are designed for you to reconsider the signing of a binding agreement (contract). Cooling-off periods change from state to state with an average of 72 hours. Some states have cooling-off periods that apply to vehicle contracts, some do not. You need to check with your state's consumer laws.

crossover:

This term is part of the sales lingo. A crossover is the changing from one aspect of negotiations to another. If the salesperson is talking about trade-in, for example, and you are stubborn about moving in the direction he wants you to go, he will change (crossover) to down payment. It is a manipulative trick to confuse and conquer. It works.

Don't let the salesperson use the crossover technique on you. Stay to one subject and complete those notes before you go on to another subject. Balk if he or she tries to intimidate you with a look that says, "What's the matter, you stupid or something?" They can't stand balking. Freeze up. Cross your arms. Refuse to budge until you understand what's happening at each aspect of the negotiations.

date of manufacture:

Finding the vehicle's build date is not always an easy task—especially on used units. I've seen many buyers find out too late that the vehicle is a year older than they thought it was. It's an old trick still used by some dealers. Be sure the year on the sales contract is the same as what the salesperson told you.

dealer-installed equipment:

Dealers make lots of money by installing equipment after the vehicle arrives from the manufacturer. Instead of averaging 20 percent profit on manufacturer-installed options, a dealer will average over 50 percent on options he installs.

If you can, avoid buying a car, truck, or RV with dealer-installed equipment. It's often overpriced and shoddily installed.

dealer prep:

Dealer preparation charges should not be considered part of the retail price unless it is part of the manufacturer's suggested retail price (MSRP). In most cases, dealer prep charges are nothing more than another way to rake the buyer over the coals. This is especially true with new RV purchases.

dealer trade:

All dealers can trade or buy vehicles from another dealer who has a franchise for the same make or brand. The dealer trade allows the buyer access to models with specific options that may not be available at the local dealership. Dealers try to avoid dealer trades because of the extra paperwork, the obligation to return the favor, and transportation costs.

dehorsing:

Dealers want to get you away from your vehicle to cement the deal. Taking you away from your "horse" and putting you on their "horse" is called dehorsing. It's an effective technique. Never allow a dealership to dehorse you for any reason until the deal is completed. Sometimes a dealer will "lose" your trade-in when trying to dehorse you. Park your vehicle where you can watch it. Keep the keys in your possession at all times.

delivery charge:

Automobiles and RVs have a legitimate delivery charge. You must be sure this charge is not altered. If you buy an RV from a manufacturer that does not provide MSRP sheets, you'll need to compare with manufacturers who do provide MSRP sheets. Actually, you shouldn't buy from any RV manufacturer who doesn't provide computer-generated MSRP sheets.

demonstrators:

Demonstrators are usually current-year vehicles driven by company personnel and salespeople. They are rarely used for demonstration purposes although they might be used for extended (and usually rough) road tests. Treat a demonstrator as a used vehicle. Be very careful about price and warranty. A tactic is to use the demo to increase "value" in a new vehicle.

If you decide to go the demo route, negotiate very carefully and watch the back-end. Be sure that the warranty has not been reduced from the standard warranty terms. Also be sure that it is not a salesman's personally owned vehicle—which may be pushed as a demo. Personally owned demos will be treated as a private-party purchase with no obligation by the dealer. The odds of getting a good deal by buying a demo is very low. (For a better deal, see "carryovers.")

deposit:

A deposit should be as small as possible and made with a personal check. Generally a personal check of $25 will get you the bottom price written on paper. Consider that after you make a good-faith deposit, you will probably be "turned" and "bumped." A deposit is always fully refundable if you decide against buying the vehicle.

depreciation:

When you drive a new vehicle off the lot, you should figure its fair-market value at 10 percent below invoice. Its actual cash value would be below that. From then on full-size cars depreciate much faster than compacts. Some appraisers compute depreciation rates after the first year with the same percentages used in the discount factors. Thus a luxury car could depreciate at 20 percent per year where a compact would depreciate at 12 percent. An RV will usually depreciate by 30 percent when driven off the lot. In the long run, however, depreciation depends much on maintenance, mileage, and demand.

discount:

I use a percent multiplier to determine the amount you should pay if a new vehicle is sold at the manufacturer's suggested retail price. Generally you can figure a multiplier ranging between .72 and .92 off the *legitimate* MSRP for autos and trucks. New RVs will range between .75 and .85 for those who show MSRP.

Because there is usually a slightly higher profit for manufacturer-installed options, the multiplier is usually lower by 3 to 5 percent. Using a multiplier makes it easier to work the figures when negotiating because you won't have to multiply then subtract as in figuring discounts.

Buying services like Consumer Reports and RV Consumer Group use multipliers to assist in advising consumers on how to negotiate.

down payment:

You might *think* you know what "down payment" means, but the dealer really *knows* what it means. To the dealer, the down payment is the heart of his entire profit. Without being able to work a down payment into a deal, the margin of profit is minimal.

A solid financial institution will usually finance 80 percent of the retail price of new vehicles. Some will only finance a percentage of the wholesale price. Used vehicles are often financed to 100 percent of the wholesale value. Everything above that amount will be needed for a down payment.

Banking institutions that provide dealers with low buy-rates may be tighter on loaning money and may loan only 80 percent of the wholesale value.

To get these low buy-rates the dealer will push qualified buyers for heavy downs to make more money on financing. With this in mind, you can realize how important it is that you shop for financing in the same manner as you shopped for the vehicle.

Because more down means more profit to the dealer, you will be constantly hit with "How much cash down can you give us?" The more sophisticated will ask, "How much are you planning for an initial investment?" They need to know so they can work you up the ladder to where the profit is the highest they can get. If you have equity in your trade-in, the salesman will still try for some cash as long as it doesn't blow the deal. If the equity in your trade will barely make the bank's requirement, the dealer must hit your billfold to increase his profit. Since a dealer always wants a minimum of 10 to 20 percent gross profit on used vehicles, you can readily see why they push hard to get you committed to more cash down.

extended service contract:

An extended service contract is provided by a company other than the manufacturer. It is generally a bad buy on new vehicles but may work on used vehicles for people who feel insecure about owning a vehicle without some sort of warranty.

Do not buy any kind of service contract unless you investigate the service underwriter. Many service contract underwriters have gone out of business leaving owners high and dry without coverage. If you don't feel comfortable with the company, don't go for it.

If you're considering a service contract, you should investigate in advance. Ask the salesperson who the underwriter is and what they get for it. Work the figures into the deal at half of what they ask for it. Always compare from dealer to dealer.

Never let a dealer tie the service contract (or service agreement) to your purchase contract without lots of thought or discussion. BEE especially loves to use the "assumptive close." He'll try to get you to thinking that service contracts, extended warranties, undercoating, and various types of insurance are normal and therefore do not need discussion. He might even seem impatient with you. It's all a ploy. It's all trickery. Don't go for this type of pressure.

factory order:

Factory orders allow you to build the car or truck to your specifications within option limits. Although a factory order has many advantages for a discriminating consumer, there are many dangers for unwary shoppers. Unscrupulous dealers may use delay tactics for a reappraisal of a trade or for claiming changes in prices or options.

If you make a factory order, be sure there is a time related cancellation clause in the agreement. (Usually about 60 days.) Do not accept a single change in the agreement. If the auto arrives with differences in price, options, or time frame from the original agreement, simply demand full refund. After the refund is in your hand, you may start over at that dealership or another. Be firm.

You should road test a factory-ordered vehicle even if you drove a similar vehicle. If it doesn't drive as you think it should, you'll need to be loud in your complaining to get your deposit back. Always keep your deposit as low as you can in case things aren't right. A small deposit gives you leverage. It's better to lose a few hundred dollars than to get stuck with a vehicle that you don't want. (Factory order deposits range from 2 to 5 percent.)

factory rebate:

Factory rebates are given to consumers and dealers. Rebates are usually given on vehicles which are overstocked for one reason or another.

fair-market value:

If you're trading your vehicle, you should never use the words "fair-market value." Fair-market value is the price you can get for it on the open market with reasonable effort. Fair-market value is in the area of what you should pay for a vehicle.

Appraisal book retail is an arbitrary figure based on what dealers would like to hold for a profit. Fair-market value will be somewhere between appraisal book retail and appraisal book wholesale. It can depend much on local-market demand.

fleet discount:

A fleet discount is usually given to buyers of three of more vehicles at one purchase. To qualify for a fleet-discount number, however, requires the purchasing of a specific number of vehicles during the year. The fleet-discount number will allow the dealer an extra discount on the vehicles which could place the purchase price below invoice. A tactic of the "good guy" salesperson is to convince buyers that he is actually selling them a vehicle at fleet discount to motivate the closing of a deal when in reality he is making a profit in excess of a fleet-discount deal.

flooring:

If you get close to a deal, the salesperson will try to convince you that his cost of keeping the vehicle on the lot makes it impossible to sell the vehicle at the price you want. He might even mention flooring.

Flooring is the monthly interest a dealer pays for financing the vehicle between the time he receives it and the time it is sold. That cost is usually between .6 percent and .75 percent per month. Some dealers "pack" the invoice with flooring and other costs. They put the total of the invoice and the pack on the inventory list as a tool for the salesperson to use against a tough buyer. Because flooring is a real overhead cost, however, it's possible to make a better deal on a newly arrived vehicle than on one that has been in stock for two or three months.

Flooring is the dealer's problem, not yours. Don't worry about the dealer. He'll make out fine.

gross profit:

This is the amount that the dealer makes above what the vehicle costs him to buy and keep to the time of sale. Auto dealers try to hold a minimum of $500 in gross profit and RV dealers try to hold a minimum of 6 percent to 10 percent. If the salesperson finds out too early that you are driving for such a deal, however, he'll stubbornly use every tactic available to keep more profit. If you have a trade, need special financing attention, or want a specific new model or used vehicle not available elsewhere, you might be forced into heavy negotiations. I must stress that learning to negotiate is a must for those of you who are discriminatory in your choice of vehicles—whether new or used.

Most of the books and videos that I have researched give the impression that the dealer is happy to get a $500 gross profit. This is bunk. A dealer wants between 10 and 20 percent of the retail as a profit on every deal.

Dealers, however, will be quick to say that this is not true. They say that they'll happily take a $500 profit. Sure they will—if they can take a trade for $1,000 below ACV, or get you to buy $1,500 of add-ons, or get you on insurance. Then what about the 3 to 5 percent hold-backs from domestic-car manufacturers? Think of it this way: A salesperson would have to sell 50 cars a month at an average of $500 gross profit to make a decent salary. No matter how you figure it, auto and RV dealers average gross profits in the two-figure percentage.

You must never feel sorry about a dealer's profit margin. There are plenty behind you who will more than make up the difference.

haggle-free dealerships:

Haggle-free dealerships claim that there's no "dealing" involved during the buying process.

Because of a current rebellion against the aggressiveness

of auto sales, haggle-free dealerships have emerged across the country. Although the concept is basically good, there are many inherent dangers for the unwary. These haggle-free dealerships still work you to buy the vehicle with the highest profit for the dealership. They manipulate trade-in values and sell heavy at financing, payment protection insurance, extended warranties, and a full line of coating protections for the vehicle. A haggle-free dealership uses the same financing tactics as does a conventional dealership.

With haggle-free dealerships, buying clubs, and buying agents, you still have to deal. Even if you have no trade, no financing, no add-ons, you still have many choices to make. Those choices are an integral part of auto dealing. Get the right information from organizations like Consumer Reports and RV Consumer Group—then use it to make good deals.

highball / lowball:

Highballs and lowballs are designed to get you back to the dealership. In a typical scenario, a salesperson will give you a price below what he or any other salesperson can sell the vehicle for. This is called a "lowball". If a trade is involved, he might give you a "highball", or high allowance, to get you to the desk or entice you to return to the dealership. The only way you can avoid being manipulated with highballs and lowballs is to know the real values of the vehicles you are considering and the ACV (actual cash value) of your trade-in.

high book:

High book is the second set of figures in an appraisal book. High book is generally shown as average retail or used retail. In order to get you to be more flexible on trade-in allowance, salespeople often will show the high book to indicate the maximum they can get for it. What they don't tell you is that the low mileage, extra equipment, and condition values are supposed to be added to the high book figure. Of course, if the mileage is abnormally high and the condition rough, your vehicle may not retail at high book. You will probably never use high book unless you sell your vehicle instead of trading it.

holdback:

Domestic dealerships receive a bonus based on volume or special models from the manufacturer called a "holdback." The holdback is usually about 3 percent of the invoice price but could vary somewhat. This amount is not reflected in the invoice or dealer cost figures. If a dealer offers you a *genuine* deal of $100 over invoice, he is relying on the holdback as his real profit in the deal. (Foreign auto and RV manufacturers do not generally have hold-backs or other incentives below invoice.)

invoice:

The invoice is the wholesale price to the dealership. Since the dealer will not sell you a vehicle without making profit, it should be clear that there could be profit below the invoice figure for domestic vehicles. This profit, however, is generated by the dealer only when the vehicle is sold. Hiding the true profit on new vehicles is easy. Hold-backs (bonuses paid by manufacturers) and other incentives are not reflected in the invoice.

lay-down:

Now that you're reading this book, you can never be a lay-down. Lay-downs are sweet, trusting souls that literally fall into the arms of the salesperson.

leader ad:

To get some idea of values for the models you have under

consideration, you will probably browse the newspapers or one of the many local publications that lists thousands of autos for sale. As you search for value, you're bound to come across some "leaders." Leaders are designed to get you into the dealership so that a salesperson can work a "bait-and-switch" scheme. Leaders are often close to the bottom price, but they can't be trusted until checked out. Some dealerships list autos with a big "special" that has been sold when you get there.

You can use leader prices to get a good idea of the bottom price. In autos, a leader is usually a stripped-down version of a popular model. The leader is often a good buy for those who want a basic model or one for a graduation gift. If you decide to buy a leader, you'll find high resistance to lowering the price, but you can tell the salesperson to include a few hundred dollars worth of options and the deal will be his. Of course, always walk away on any leader deal if there's any question. Use caution on the walk, however, because there is usually a time limit and often a number limit for the sale. I know people who wait for leaders once they make up their minds to buy a particular make and model. If you are an impulse buyer, however, you might fall into the trap by going to inspect a leader and getting switched.

license estimate:

When you get your registration, be sure to check the figures with your sales contract. Some dealers are quick to give high license estimates but forget to give you a refund for overcharges.

limited production:

A limited production or special edition model is usually a test for the manufacturer's marketing department. If it has radical changes, you should be aware that parts and services may also be limited if and when it is discontinued.

liner:

Many dealerships have greeters that are also called liners. The job of the liner is to line you up for a Smoothy closer. The liner will introduce you to a vehicle, qualify you, give a presentation on the lot and on a demonstration ride, and dump you in the office. Liners get their commission on the end result—so they'll work hard to set you up well.

Trust begins at the greeting. It is a known fact that if a professional salesperson greets and qualifies in a friendly and candid manner, 80 percent of his prospects will give him a good portion of trust. (That's **80** percent!) This is the beginning of being taken to the cleaners. Trusting an unknown person for guidance in spending your hard-earned cash is indeed a foolhardy act.

low book:

Normally considered the base wholesale of an auto, truck, or RV. You must keep in mind that base wholesale is without adding for extra equipment and condition or subtracting for condition and mileage. If the salesperson bases his evaluation on low book instead of full wholesale, he's taking you to the cleaners.

lowball:

A lowball is a figure below the price the dealer can actually sell a vehicle. A lowball is used often to get you back to the dealership when you're in a shopping mode. Using a lowball is a common trick.

MSRP:

MSRP stands for manufacturer's suggested retail price. Automobile and truck dealers are forced by law (Monroney Act) to have a manufacturer's suggested retail price sheet (Monroney label) on every new vehicle — until it is delivered to a retail buyer. RV dealers are not required to do so at the time of this writing.

The only practical way of buying a vehicle is discounting off MSRP. If you use this as a basis for shopping, it will work on any item that shows a *genuine* MSRP. Once you get a wholesale figure for any model of any make or brand, you can compute discount and get wholesale figures on any other similar model. Simply divide the invoice figure by the MSRP and you'll have your multiplying factor. In this way you won't get confused by different equipment or other options installed at the factory. Take the MSRP, multiply by the multiplying factor, and you'll have the dealer cost based on invoice. The rest is easy. All you have to decide is how much of your valuable money you want the dealer to keep as his profit. Personally, under the current operating rules, I would never give a car or truck dealer over $500 or an RV dealer over 10 percent of the MSRP above the dealer cost figure. (Remember, auto and truck dealers get hold-backs.)

The Monroney Act does not stop the dealers from making excessive profits. They constantly come up with new tricks to waylay uninformed buyers. They attach dealer price labels right next to the MSRP sheet. Many buyers will use it as a price reference.

Dealers are experts at getting you to see the figure they want you to see. They do it many times every day. They raise the price $3,000 and discount it $2,000. They can make the supplementary label look "government like" to get you to think it's official. They can make the asking price big to get you to think it's a good deal.

There is only one way to price a vehicle: *Use the figures on the MSRP sheet.* You have to be careful with RVs because many so-called MSRP sheets are not genuine. (RV Consumer Group can help you here.)

NMI:

New model introductions (NMI) are usually preceded by manufacturer and dealer promos to get you excited. Bargaining on new models is usually rough for the first 60 days. A good policy is, "Go see, don't buy." If you are committed or determined to buy a new model introduction, be prepared for hard bargaining.

numbers game:

When you learn to work the system, you'll discover that some dealerships will push for the sale even at a low profit. The reason these dealerships push for numbers is threefold. 1) They want to rotate inventory to keep it fresh. 2) They know the percentages—the higher the volume the more high-profit sales. 3) They make a tremendous profit with after-sale services. Your objective should be to give a dealership the least profit it will accept for a particular vehicle. To get to this point, you need to do comparative shopping on new and research for the actual cash value on used. If you don't do these things, you will fall into the trap of adding another gold star to the sales manager's monthly report.

offer:

If you decide you want to go right to the bottom on a new vehicle, you'll have to play the "offer" game carefully. You'll need to negotiate hard with at least two dealerships. I repeat: **You must negotiate hard with at least two dealerships.** This is often difficult because most dealerships won't deal to the bottom unless you are quite committed to buying on that day. If you negotiate without a commitment to buy, figure that you'll be about 2 percent of the sticker price above the bottom. Of course, this will vary with the amount of enthusiasm and expertise you use in the negotiating. But if the two figures are quite close, you can assume that you are sitting on the edge of a good deal.

Many otherwise good shoppers simply walk into a dealership after getting a "bottom price" at another dealership. Let's suppose you visit two dealerships under this method and get a bottom price of $13,895 at one and $13,875 at the other. You go to the third dealership and offer to pay $13,675 for the exact model on which you got the two prices. The third dealer tries to bump you but finally accepts the deal at your offer if you buy right then. What you didn't know is that the first two dealerships were holding a few percentage points above the bottom price. They might have had confidence that the salesperson could get you back with a sweetener. Most dealers are too smart to drop to the bottom unless they are convinced they will lose the deal. I know many buyers who use the offer system in this example and invariably throw away between $300 and $1,000 dollars. There is no easy way to get to the bottom of the pot.

optional equipment:

Optional equipment is all the equipment that does not come with the vehicle's base price. Theoretically, you should be able to use any vehicle without a single piece of optional equipment. There are two types of optional equipment: 1) factory installed, and 2) dealer installed. As a general rule, factory-installed equipment is a much better value than dealer installed equipment. (See "add-ons.")

out-the-door:

Out-the-door price includes taxes and license. An out-the-door price should be the same as the total of the sales contract.

over-allowance:

The over-allowance is the amount allowed for a trade-in less its actual cash value. A better way to deal is to accept the actual cash value as if it were hard cash and negotiate the price of the vehicle being purchased on a no-trade basis. Another term for over-allowance is "packing the trade."

packed-for-bear:

Salespeople hate buyers who come to the dealership packed-for-bear. Packed-for-bear means having the equipment (big guns) to do the job. When you're packed-for-bear, you'll have pens, notepad, calculator, and a folder full of information. You'll want to appear as a serious buyer, but you do not want to give the appearance that you are ready to take on the dealership.

In your folder you'll have brochures or pamphlets normally given as handouts. You will have them marked with any questions that you need answered. You should always have some questions about the warranty. You would want to be clear on engine size, fuel economy factors, specifications, exterior colors, interior colors, and optional equipment. All of this should be behind you before you sit down to negotiate. Your goal will be to keep the negotiating session as short and smooth as possible.

For car, truck, or RV buying, I prefer a folder to a briefcase because the folder will limit the amount of information you take to a specific dealership. That's right. **You need to limit the paperwork you take with you during shopping or negotiating.** Take only the information that's pertinent to the makes you will be discussing. Everything else stays in the car or at home. Things like your state's lemon laws are important to you—but not to the dealership. Having the competition's advertising along will only throw a rotting tomato in the ring to absorb valuable time. You need to keep the focus where it belongs — on the product.

Salespeople try all the tricks on buyers packed-for-bear. You'll have to remember everything I've said about trusting auto salespeople. They'll try to turn and bump you until they make the deal or let you walk. Some salespeople have no patience with a packed-for-bear buyer.

packing the sticker:

A trick of the trade is to add a bit into the computations when you first begin to negotiate. If the salesperson gets caught, he will call it a pack. "Oh, this $200 is our service pack," he'll say. You must remember that all negotiations begin with and stay with the MSRP—not a blown-up figure. If you're dealing on a used vehicle, the pack would be above the dealer retail figure on the inventory sheet, the price posted on the vehicle, or a price quoted in an ad. Consider that packing the sticker by $200 will get the salesperson a $50 bonus. Carrying your $10 calculator will help eliminate packing the sticker.

payment ad:

A payment ad is designed to reach payment buyers. It is usually misleading. The low payment figure will invariably depend upon the amount of trade-in value or down payment. It also depends on the duration of the loan. Thus the fine print will actually be saying, "If you come in with enough down and don't mind a term that is longer than the vehicle will last, you will get the low payment *if* the financial institution approves the loan." Don't believe payment ads!

payment buyer:

There's never been such a love affair as between an auto salesperson and a payment buyer. Like a good lover, an auto salesperson will twist a payment buyer this way and that way until they get exactly what they want. They have literally hundreds of tricks for payment buyers. From the first time you respond positively to mention of payment, they use two words: "payment" and "today".

You must not get caught in the payment game until you find the car and get the bottom price. This means that you must have some idea what you can handle in payments before you go to the dealership. You must check with banks and credit union. It's all free. They encourage your research. You can do it by phone.

You should always know the percentage of your expenses to your income before you apply for financing. When you total your expenses, include all fixed payments. Divide that figure by your income and you'll have the percentage of expense to income. If that percentage is over 40 percent you might have some difficulty getting financed even if you have good credit.

To arrive at a figure you can afford as a monthly payment, you need to do some homework. Some guidelines for payment buyers are as follows: 1) You should not increase your payment if your expense-to-income percentage is in the 40 percent or higher range. 2) If you are in the 30 to 40 percent range, you should use caution in increasing your payment. 3) If you are below 30 percent, you are generally safe to increase your payment to about 35 percent of that ratio. These are guidelines—they are not foolproof.

You should be prepared for paying dearly if the auto dealer holds the paper, backs the loan, or uses clout to get the financing approved. In such a scenario, you'll pay more for the vehicle, you'll be subject to a higher interest rate, and you'll be pressured for every back-end service the dealership pushes. I have seen many cases where the total cost for the vehicle almost doubled because the dealer controlled the financing.

Since loaning institutions do not generally like to loan money to those who have been turned down elsewhere, walk carefully if your credit is borderline. There are many ways you can research your financing potential without consulting with the hawks. Protect your financial future. Learning now how to handle your personal financing will get you better deals for the rest of your life.

If you have your own financing or are paying cash, there's no reason to tell the salesperson about it. He'll want you to be a payment buyer, so go along with his dreams. Don't lie, just use "maybe" a lot. Keep the salesperson motivated into getting to an acceptable bottom figure. Be firm that you want to negotiate the price before you talk financing. You can even sign all the papers, give the down payment, and leave financing open for a specific number of days. Be sure it's all clear on the purchase contract. Don't let them say, "It's understood, we don't have to write it on the contract." It must be clear that you have a specific number of days for choosing a specific method of paying. If it takes a hundred-word paragraph, that's okay. They can always add a page.

preliminary research:

Auto salespeople are trained to satisfy wants. They are programmed to pump your emotions. Salespeople around the world are trained to manipulate you like a puppet. They thrive on books, videos, seminars, and workshops that instruct them in the art of manipulation. Not one of these selling aids emphasizes satisfying needs.

Some salespeople will try to influence you by building a balance sheet to show the advantages and disadvantages of a model under consideration. Listen carefully, then put the sheet in your folder or pocket without asking for permission to do so. Because many salespeople have good information about their products, give them a chance to show their knowledge; but study the information at home while building your own balance sheet.

The only way you're going to find out what's on the market is to visit auto dealerships. To get good information from a salesperson, you need to be a friendly sponge who is buying in the near future. If you want answers, you must be loose and friendly. The goal of the salesperson is to catch you while you're there. Your goal is to collect information and get out. Since most salespeople operate by rote, you are almost guaranteed 30 minutes of information if your attitude is right and you play the game.

pre-owned:

Pre-owned means "used." Buying used is totally different from buying new because no two used vehicles are even close to being the same. Mileage, condition, equipment, colors, and maintenance history are important factors when considering buying used. Because I am generally a used-vehicle buyer, I learned years ago to negotiate hard when I am sure the vehicle is close to what I want and need. This works equally well with private-party purchases or dealerships.

With used, try it in three steps. 1) After you've gone through the appraisal process, negotiate hard to try to get to a figure well below what you think they'll accept. 2) Leave the desk for another look at the vehicle. 3) Return to the desk with your offer.

When you try to accomplish step two of this three-step system, you'll be surprised at the resistance you'll encounter. The salesperson won't want you to go because he or she will figure they'll never see you again. If you've shown you can live without the vehicle, the salesperson at this time might go to the bottom. Don't tell the salesperson how much you like the vehicle. Tell him that it'll satisfy your needs. Every auto salesperson knows that basic needs can be satisfied at almost any auto sales lot.

presentation:

You should always consider that 90 percent of what the salesperson tells you during a presentation is either guesswork or outright lies. "I toured the factory where they build this baby and I tell you that I never saw better craftsmanship anywhere," is close to what you'll often hear from RV and auto salespeople. In the first place, few of these salespeople would know craftsmanship if they saw it. In the second place, few salespeople go on such tours.

Notice how sincere and enthusiastic a salesperson is as he opens and closes doors. Notice how he points out the streamlined dash and safety features. All of this is to mesmerize you. He doesn't want you studying the MSRP sheet with standard and optional equipment. He definitely doesn't want you to get figures fixed in your brain. He'll maintain control by pointing to frivolous features—staying away from technical specifics.

The best way to learn about a vehicle's features is to spend some time alone in the vehicle with a brochure in hand.

prime-time buying:

There are times when it's easier to make a deal than others. Daily: usually mid-afternoon. Weekly: Monday and weekends for fast deals—midweek for slower dealing. Monthly: near beginning and near end because contests are usually intense at that time. Holidays: Some are good but most buyers make bad deals at Christmas time. Yearly: Usually best between New Year's and Spring.

In all cases, the edge is probably slight because smart buyers get good deals anytime.

promo:

A promo is an advertising blitz designed to increase floor traffic. Generally the costs of promos is figured on the number of deals written into the dollars spent on the promo. Promos can cost anywhere from $25 to $200 for each prospect brought to the desk. The sole purpose of a promo is to "hook 'em and fry 'em." Watch out for hyped salespeople at promo time.

(Also see "leader ad".)

qualifying:

When you approach a vehicle on an auto sales lot, a salesperson will probably be watching your every move. He or she will have a unique way of approaching you to keep your guard down. Salespeople want you in a relaxed mode so they can qualify you quickly without you knowing what's happening. They are trained to get certain questions answered within a specific period of time. If the salesperson is good at what he's doing, it will take only a few minutes to get enough information to begin leading you by the nose. Don't kid yourself. This is the way it works.

During the qualifying process (which continues throughout the demonstration) the salesperson is mentally calculating how much you'll tolerate as a payment. This is the key to auto sales. The salesperson wants a payment buyer because he or she knows that payment buyers will usually pay more and will go for optional equipment that produces much higher profits. He also knows that payment buyers are more apt to go for insurance and other high profit services.

If you want to take advantage of the salesperson's hunger for a deal, lead him with a few statements and questions of your own. A simple opening statement to get a salesperson's adrenaline flowing is, "I would like to look at your (specific model)." "Are you able to handle my financing?" will get him enthusiastic about the presentation. "If I buy a (car, truck, RV) from you, will you...?" will start him thinking that you are a serious buyer.

repos:

Repossessions, or "repos," are always dangerous to buy unless the price is at least 20 percent below normal retail. Repossessed vehicles are generally more abused than traded vehicles. You should also consider that repossessed vehicles are bought 20 to 30 percent back of book (below wholesale) by the dealer. If you suspect that the vehicle could be a repossession, have the dealer give you a statement that it is not a repossession. You can also ask for the previous owner's name and address.

road test:

An auto dealer is generous with allowing you to road test a car, truck, or RV because it works at getting you to the desk. Some salespeople will toss you the keys with hardly a question because they know the percentages—and the cost doesn't come from their commissions. Sometimes they're busy with another customer and it's a good way to keep their prospect busy until they get free. Most salespeople, however, will qualify you before the road test. If they ride with you and become the nice guy, you'll have a tough time saying "No" to a reasonable deal. By making it a "demonstration ride" the odds for a sale are dramatically increased. They know it works because they've tested their system thousands of times.

During a demonstration ride, you might be taken through a rundown commercial or residential section of town so you'll feel better about the car you're driving. Most salespeople will chatter very lightly about the wonderful features of the car, truck, or RV as they ride with you. This is when they'll try to become your friend.

Some salespeople will ask you to check out "your new car" to be sure everything works. They want you to think of it as "your new car" when you enter negotiations. As you drive into the dealership, you might be asked to park in an area reserved for sold vehicles.

As soon as you get back on the lot, any good sales manager will demand that the salesperson gets you to his or her desk. If the road test didn't have the desired effect, they'll want the salesperson to tell them why.

During the small talk about the vehicle in question, you'll be inched into negotiating. They'll want you to deal. They'll want you into their territory. They'll want you to think you hold all the cards. They'll want you to think this way because it gets your guard down. They know the system. They know their closing rate. They play the odds every day.

Smoothy:

The Smoothy salesperson is the biggest danger to the car buyer. A Smoothy salesperson will think of you as a piece of machinery that walks into his life. Smoothies are the best of manipulators. They have the most tricks up their sleeves. They are silver tongued. The number one trick of a Smoothy is to appear as a beginner. It gives him (or her) a chance to recover from "mistakes" or "claims." The dealer goes along with this because it's been in the system for a long time.

If you're a smart buyer and you still get caught, you've met a Smoothy.

split:

Salespeople try hard to prevent splitting a commission with another salesperson or closer. If you want the salesperson to fight for you while keeping away from a split, tell him up front that you won't take a turnover to another salesperson. Say, "If you and I can't get together on a deal, I'm gone." You can also tell the salesperson that you have a time limitation. Say, "I've about an hour left to get this deal together. If we can't do it now, I'll have to come back." The salesperson always wants it done *now*.

standard equipment:

This is the equipment that comes with a specific model and is included in the base price. Generally, standard equipment

cannot be dropped or exchanged.

sticker price:

Sticker price is not the same as Manufacturer's Suggested Retail Price (MSRP). Sticker price usually is the figure the dealer attaches to the vehicle. You don't want sticker price — you want MSRP.

The dealer can put any price he wants on the vehicle, but the MSRP with all equipment and identifying data must be left on all new cars and trucks. Leaving the manufacturer's price sheet on the vehicle is mandated by law for your protection.

Don't get in the habit of saying, "sticker price." The salesperson will use this terminology because he'll want you to be thinking supplementary sticker price—which includes dealer added equipment and services. You must not think that way. You must think, "MSRP means manufacturer's suggested retail price." If you think this way, you'll automatically save money on every deal you negotiate.

When the salesperson talks sticker price, retail price, or selling price, always respond with, "manufacturer's suggested retail price" and be sure you know what it is.

straight-sell house:

A straight-sell house may allow the greeting salesperson to take the deal all the way to its conclusion. Some straight-sell houses even allow the salesperson to handle back-end services. Straight-sell houses, however, are less than 20 percent of the total auto sales market. Most RV dealerships are straight-sell houses, but turnover houses are increasing.

You will rarely find an amateur in a straight-sell house. Most straight-sell house salespeople come from auto dealerships, real estate agencies, or door-to-door sales. The tricks of the trade come with them. If the salesperson has worked in a system house or turnover house, you can bet he'll have hundreds of tricks waiting for you.

You can still be bumped and turned in a straight-sell house. In most cases, you'll find the salesperson making many trips to his "boss" or the sales manager. He'll want you to know that he's the "good guy" and the unknown person in some back office is the tough guy. He might work with a worksheet or a computer. He might work with both. Straight-sell houses allow the personality of the salesperson to dominate the negotiations—as long as his average profit is acceptable.

I highly recommend working with a straight-sell house. By their very nature, system and turnover houses take a heavy mental and physical toll. With a straight-sell house, you get to know the salesperson enough to build a strategy.

switch:

Salespeople switch buyers all the time. They switch them to the models with bonuses and "spiffs." They switch them to models with add-ons. They switch them from price to payments. They switch them from trading their old car to selling it on their own. They switch them from credit unions to dealer financing. They are always switching you from saying "No!" to saying "Yes!" Switching is an art for an auto, truck, or RV salesperson.

I personally know of an auto dealer who switched an old man from the car he wanted to a car with an MSRP of $2,000 less—while paying the same price. The old man paid cash, and when I saw him he was very unhappy with the car he bought. The dealer stood firm on the deal. When I went to arbitrate, I did my loud-voice arbitration standing in the center of the showroom floor. The old man got the right car only when the dealer realized that it was going to cost him much more than the profits on that one car.

You may think it's easy to avoid switching, but don't be

fooled. If done correctly, it's very subtle. If you catch the switch, the salesperson may try the "shock treatment" to get you to go along. Something like, "I hate to tell you this, John, but that car will probably be out of your budget. This one should fit perfectly, and there's little difference." If you still want the first car, he'll know you're ready for a bump on the payment.

When he's trying to switch you from a credit union, he may use something like, "Credit unions limit the amount of loans to individual members. If you use them for buying a car, the money won't be available for something else that's more difficult to finance through banks." He'll talk about credit union controls and red tape. He'll switch from one subject to another until you say, "Yes!"

trade-in:

Most people use a vehicle for the down payment on the purchase of another vehicle. Deep down in our guts, all of us know that we're losing many dollars by trading the vehicle rather than selling it on our own; but we think it's the most practical thing to do. We might have come to the conclusion that the vehicle we have is seriously flawed or that we're not capable of selling it ourselves. Even though most buyers know that auto dealers make between 25 and 50 percent profit on every used vehicle they sell, many are determined to use it as a trade-in.

The biggest mistake buyers make is to allow the trade to enter negotiations before you settle on a vehicle. You must not do this. It's easy to figure the equity in your trade. Simply find the ACV and deduct your payoff. The equity can be used as all or part of the down payment.

Dealers like trade-ins because they can play the numbers game. If they have their way, they may even make more profit on the trade than they make on the new vehicle. By playing the numbers game they can make the figures on the worksheets look good to the buyer. The numbers game gets into scaring and confusing the buyer. This is the dirty tricks part of many auto sales businesses.

I have seen many salespeople drool over a trade-in even as they attempt to convince the prospect that the vehicle is seriously flawed or not in demand. I have seen salespeople use service personnel to help them with the pitch. I have often seen service people exaggerate and even lie to get a $20 bill in their pocket. This tactic works well on women and older people. It's easy. It's profitable.

When a prospect is convinced that his vehicle has serious problems and then is given a generous figure for a trade-in, the barriers evaporate. If the trust game is played from the beginning, the numbers game will usually win. Unless you understand how the figures work, you are playing blind even if you negotiate hard. The people you are working against have many years of collective experience to use against you. It is rarely a hostile atmosphere; but when it gets down to the close, that can also develop. The whole game is to milk you dry.

When you study about discounts in this glossary, you should realize that although the ACV of your trade-in won't change, the trade-in allowance could change as you switch vehicle categories. For example, if you go from a compact to a pickup, you could have a substantial increase in trade-in allowance. This, of course, will depend on whether you follow the procedure advised under the term "trade-in allowance".

Never sign a title before the contract is signed. If they ask for your title before the trade is signed, you may show it but *never* let it out of your sight. Salespeople often *misplace* titles and keys to keep the prospect from walking.

trade-in allowance:

The trade-in allowance is the amount the dealer will allow for your trade on the purchase contract. The allowance can be either the list price less a trade-in allowance, or the discounted price less actual cash value (ACV) of the trade-in.

When you use list less a trade-in allowance figure, you may have a problem keeping up with the manipulative tactics of a good salesperson. If you negotiate the purchase price and then negotiate the trade, you have, in essence, two negotiating sessions. Believe it or not, this is the easiest way for most buyers. By using a three-step negotiating method, you will deal with 1) purchase price, 2) trade-in allowance, and 3) finance—in that order. You must understand, however, that the salesperson will not want this to happen. He will invariably try to tie everything together with one knot. (See "switch.")

trade-or-sell agreement:

If you are ordering a new vehicle, you can almost always work a trade-or-sell agreement with the dealer. Both figures will be locked into the agreement which will allow you to try to sell the vehicle on your own. If the dealer resists this agreement, he is looking at your trade as valuable merchandise which tells you the trade deal is not in your favor. I recommend doing the trade deal only after you have worked hard at negotiating a no-trade deal. Use the trade-or-sell agreement deal as a last ditch effort by saying, "I'll place the order if you agree to take my trade at wholesale (or actual cash value) if I can't sell it." Of course, then you'll have to be sure that the trade-in figure is acceptable.

A trade-or-sell agreement works well when factory ordering a vehicle.

trial close:

If the salesperson thinks you are either a shopper or incapable of buying, he will skirt a good presentation by making statements to get you to the desk. This is called a trial close.

turn:

The turn (or turnover) is a process of switching you to another salesperson at some point in the negotiations. Unless the dealership is a system-house or turnover house, the point of turnover is left to the salesperson or sales manager. Turnover houses are dealerships that specialize in two, three, and even four turnovers before the buyer is closed or allowed to walk.

When turned, you will be facing a fresh opponent. This new face can test the waters by claiming ignorance of the facts or by making the previous salesperson appear incompetent. His mind will be uncluttered while yours will be cluttered.

If you are an easy-sell with lots of profit in the deal, many dealerships still require a turn and a "bump". In some dealerships the structure is firm. Whether you are a smart shopper or an easy-sell, you could be turned to a closer then to a sales manager. Through hook or crook, most dealerships will go for every penny they can get.

turn-on words:

The Smoothies in the auto and RV industries have a good understanding of the American buying psyche. They know that for most Americans money comes easy but saving is hard. They know that most of us have been oriented to a world of investing rather than saving. They know we have been taught that investing is adventuresome where saving is prudent. They know that being prudent is not something most Americans want to brag about. Because Americans respond to certain words, the Smoothies in the auto industry have a ready-made language for their games.

Smoothies learn to use certain words. They call these words 'turn-ons'. These are words and phrases that push the emotion buttons in almost everybody. Sale, invest, special, safe, save, opportunity, efficient, pleasant, super, fantastic, fully reconditioned, great buy, good deal, guarantee, and easy are some words that auto salespeople learn to use to encourage buying signals. You can be almost sure that the phrases "I can fit this into your budget " and "I'm on your side" will be used to get you to the desk.

"Today" is the biggest trick word used by auto, truck, and RV dealers. By using this word often, they will build a sense of urgency and get you thinking their way. "If I can do this today, will you buy today?" "Are you ready to do business today?" "If I can get you into this vehicle at the right price, are you willing to drive it home today?" "We have a special price on this vehicle today." "In order to win the contest, I must have one more sale today." "This interest rate is good only today." The "today" statements used by salespeople can literally fill a book.

In themselves using "turn-on" words and phrases is not trickery. Every person who courts another uses button-pushers at one time or another. Preachers, politicians, teachers, doctors, lawyers, and all parents learn to use certain words to set a mood or get a reaction. Most people, however, have placed limitations on the use of these words. These limits are based on honesty and integrity. Auto salespeople have a reputation for disregarding all limits. To prove this you need only to study the auto advertising of television, radio, and newspaper. Auto salespeople will usually agree that this is a real condition of the trade, but it's always the other person who fits the description.

upside down:

A person is upside down when he owes more on the vehicle than it is worth. Being upside down makes trading or selling very difficult.

vehicle longevity:

A new vehicle is not necessarily a good vehicle. Many cars and trucks have been discontinued because the public finally woke up to discover that they were junk from their inception. This is sad but factual. Most auto manufacturers have built bad cars and trucks. Most RV manufacturers still build bad models. Many of us who claim to be intelligent buyers have purchased these vehicles. We bought them because we were convinced that the purchase would make our lives more secure and our lifestyle more exciting. We were indoctrinated into trusting the system.

Buying the right vehicle is not difficult. We know, for example, that if we want a small economy car or truck that will last for 200,000 miles and still be solid enough to pass on to another family member, we'll have to include foreign makes in our consideration. Much of the value of a trade will depend upon the vehicle's reputation for longevity.

walk:

This is a good word for buyers. It's a word that salespeople hate to hear. Dealers do, however, have many tricks to keep you from "walking."

Most car and truck buyers don't realize that walking is their best defense when the going gets rough. The salesperson's goal from the beginning is to control the prospect's footsteps. Controlling the prospect's feet is an awesome skill—one that many auto salespeople have.

Keep your feet loose. Don't let them get tired. Keep them synchronized with your mouth. If you say that you want to look at another vehicle, let your feet begin to move. If you say that you'd like to see the specs on a vehicle, let your feet take you to the display area. If you say that you need to leave, let your feet start walking to the exit. Your feet will carry the rest of you away from a situation that's getting out of control.

If you are an impulse buyer, you must rely on your feet more than most. Impulse buyers need to use their feet to retreat because their heads can't stop nodding. They can leave their checkbooks at home and the dealership will still win the day. Impulse buyers are easy to "dehorse." With their car at the dealership and the dealership's car fitting nicely around their body, impulse buyers are doomed. They usually get some of the worst deals recorded. Impulse buyers usually buy the wrong vehicle at the wrong price.

I must emphasize that most people have a hard time walking away. If you find yourself wanting to be the nice guy by helping the salesperson get a well-earned commission, bonus, or trip, you are not abnormal. The salesperson is becoming your friend. He definitely knows something about the auto business that you don't. He knows that you need him, and you know that you need him. If there's no chemistry, there's no problem anyway. No smart buyer will buy a car or truck from a salesperson they don't trust. When the trust is there, it's really hard to say, "No." But if you want to win, say it with your feet.

What About RV Buying?

There are differences in buying a car or truck and buying a recreational vehicle. Throughout my studies of the RV industry, I have discovered that the unregulated RV industry is blatantly indifferent to consumerism. It is not only the dog-eat-dog atmosphere within the industry, but the dog-eat-mouse attitude towards the RV buyer. Because most RVs are built in large "barns" across the country, it is the most haphazard business I have ever seen. Thousands of RVs are built every year that should not be classified as anything except crackerboxes. Even the best manufacturers are building models that are unsafe and destined to be short-lived.

When I began designing the computer program for RV Consumer Group in 1993 to analyze the over 10,000 RV models being produced every year, I could not have imagined the resulting data. According to information collected from manufacturer's brochures, close to 50 percent of all models have serious deficiencies in build specifications alone. When you top this information with data from investigative reports of new RVs and appraisals of used RVs, the result is most discouraging.

Our analysis begins by inputting seventy pieces of information. This information includes size specifications, weight factors, power factors, fuel capacities, holding tank capacities, suspension data, and house-build data. To get the right data into the computer, we study brochures, we call the manufacturers, and we visit local dealerships for inspections.

Many manufacturers purposely omit information from the brochures that could interfere with marketing. Information like payload capacities and gross weights are often omitted because they are deficient or excessive. Because government regulations are almost nonexistent for recreational vehicles, the manufacturer's conscience alone determines build characteristics relating to safety and performance.

With all this in mind, you should realize that you alone cannot conclude which RV brand or model is safe or reliable. Without help, determining which of the hundreds of brands and thousands of models to eliminate from your search is just about impossible. If I cannot do it without the help of a professional staff and a well-packed computer, how can you?

The manufacturers and dealerships know all of this. They see the frustration from buyers every day. They know how to work the frustration into the emotions. They know the key words and phrases. They know how to put brochures together and how to market to the emotions. They don't want informed buyers.

You can beat them at their game, but it's not as easy as with a car or truck. Because most RV dealerships are now using auto-selling techniques, the dealing part is about the same. The difference is in the choosing.

The first thing you need to realize is that there are no RV experts on the sales lots. Most RV salespeople don't want to know anything beyond the very basics. Most RV salespeople work at the trade because they want the good commissions. Like the auto salespeople, most will say anything to get those commissions. At RV Consumer Group we get input from our members. They share their experiences with us. They tell how the various dealerships treat them. We get stories about manipulations, about low-balls, about playing with trade figures. The stories go on and on. As our computer composes the picture, we get a new view of RV selling methods across the country.

The only way to buy an RV in this atmosphere is to be part of an information-sharing program. RV Consumer Group alone offers this service. Its volunteer and participating members crisscross the country via wheels and phones to compile data for this program. With this information you can begin to make decisions.

Because buying an RV is an emotional act, no amount of information will guarantee you making the right choice. An article in an RV trade magazine emphasized that RV salespeople use turn-on words to work on your emotions. Like the auto industry, the RV industry is getting rich with manipulative tactics.

So don't let it get to you. Get informed and stay cool. Don't let any signs of urgency show. Keep your emotions in your hip pocket or purse. Walk away to cool down if necessary. Most of all, join RV Consumer Group and start the process with its membership program.

jd gallant

Pledge

I will not negotiate until I know exactly what I want and how much it will cost me. I will not talk finances until all other conditions are settled.

Five Rules

1. KNOW YOUR ENEMY.
2. KEEP THEM OUT OF YOUR POCKETS.
3. DON'T TRUST THEM FOR A MOMENT.
4. BE BOLD, BE CAUTIOUS, AND BE FAST ON YOUR FEET.
5. DON'T TAKE IT IN THE BACK-END.

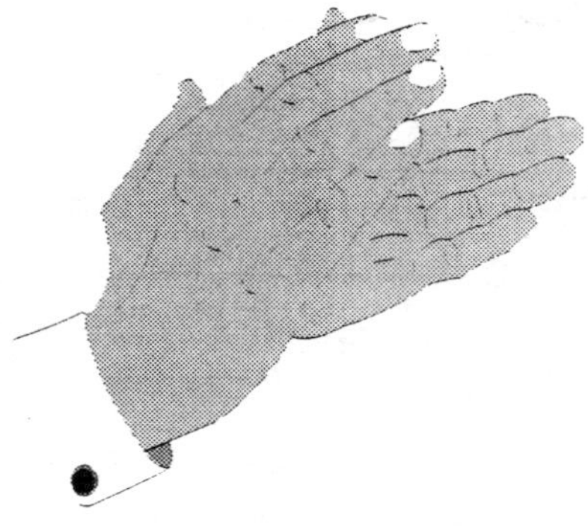

This handclap is for ***you***!

Congratulations —

you've done yourself a great service by reading this book.

jd gallant